COLORADO FOURTEENERS

POCKET SLAM

Contents

Fort Collins, Colorado

Disclaimer

Climbing mountains can be dangerous. The author assumes no liability for the actions of any reader. While the attempt has been made to be accurate, the directions may contain errors of fact. Almost certainly directions can be misinterpreted. It is impossible for the author to anticipate all the various skill levels of people who might purchase this book. Therefore, the author does not offer this book to the consumer for any purpose other than pleasure reading.

Published by: Above the Timber
2366 Wapiti Road
Fort Collins, Colorado 80525

Design and Page Layout: Roger Edrinn
Typesetting: TeleTech Typesetting, Fort Collins, CO
Printed by: Citizen Printing, Fort Collins, CO

Library of Congress CCN 91-70372
ISBN 1-56044-088-0

Cover Photo: The scenic high trail to Capitol Lake about 4 miles from Capitol Peak. The low trail follows Capitol Creek below and left.

Forward

Hopefully all of the information in ***Pocket Slam*** will be obvious by the context, some explanation may answer a few doubts.

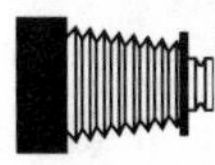

Refers to my two photo books on the *COLORADO FOURTEENERS* ***GRAND SLAM*** and ***THE 54 HIGHEST PEAKS***. The numbers relate to pages which have photos of the associated summit. Not all of these photos will aid in a climb, but all are shown for completeness.

Each climbing route is shown with a symbol showing its relative climbing difficulty:

- ♦♦ Very Difficult
- ♦ Difficult
- ■ Moderate
- ● Easy

Further, each route has the round-trip elevation gain and distance. Of these the elevation gain is by far the better indicator of effort needed to conquer one of the fourteeners. For approaches the elevation gain and distance are shown as one-way measurements.

Both elevation gain and distance are shown from the end of the car road instead of the 4WD road. While 4WD roads may shorten any route, the reader is left to calculate the elevation savings from the text. Do not confuse all-wheel-drive with 4WD, AWD vehicles lack necessary ground clearance and gearing.

Because of the many combinations of routes and summits it was not possible to be absolutely consistent in presentation. In all cases I attempted the best possible information in the most logical and concise manner. Enjoy!!!

Roger Edrinn

Longs Peak

14,255

From the Top: Perhaps the largest summit of all the fourteeners, Longs is surrounded on all sides by steep cliffs. To the west is an unbroken ridge of mountains which form the Continental Divide in northern Colorado. Evidence of the carving power of ice age glaciers can be seen all along this high ridge. Several mountain parks (mountain enclosed meadows) can be seen to the north, including Moraine, Horseshoe and Estes Parks.

Grand Slam: 1, 12, 13
54 Highest: 14

Longs Peak Ranger Station

The Longs Peak campground turnoff is 8 miles south of Estes Park on CO-7. Drive west .5 mile to the Longs Peak Ranger Station, 9400 feet. Three route choices start from the parking lot.

Register at the trailhead booth and hike west 4 miles to Chasm Lake Junction, 11,550 feet. For the Keyhole and Cable routes continue on the right fork NW to Granite Pass, 12,050 feet, and turn SW to the base of the Boulder Field, 12,600 feet.

Keyhole ◆

Elevation Gain: **5100 feet** Distance: **18 miles**

The Boulder Field contains boulders bigger than a car and the route goes over them WSW to The Keyhole, 13,150 feet. The Keyhole formation has a tremendous overhang and it is a tribute to the strength of Longs Peak's granite that it doesn't come crashing down.

Starting at the Keyhole the route is marked by 'fried eggs,' painted red circles with yellow centers. From the Keyhole go up then down on a series of rock shelves, along Longs' west face, to The Trough, 13,100 feet. The Trough is a steep gravel gully which leads SE to a gap, 13,900 feet, between the summit and The Keyboard of the Winds. The Narrows, a solid, exposed ledge section, leads east on the south face to the Home Stretch. The Home Stretch is 300 feet of great steep rock which can be two-pointed its entire length to the summit. Most climbers will prefer to three and four-point this section. Amazingly the summit is enormous, rivaling Bross and Pikes in area.

Cable Route ♦♦

Elevation Gain: **4900 feet** Distance: **16 miles**

From the Boulder Field hike SE toward the steep north face just right of The Diamond. About one hundred yards west of The Diamond a steep staircase of rock, only without any stairs, has several large steel eye-bolts embedded into the wall. These used to have a steel cable threaded through them, hence the name. It is possible to friction climb this section to a series of steep chutes which lead directly to the summit. Technical training is a must for this route and the Park Service may require you to register as a technical climb.

Loft and Palisades ♦♦

Elevation Gain: **5100 feet** Distance: **16 miles**

From Chasm Lake Junction survey the grassy gully, east of Ships Prow, leading to the saddle between Mount Meeker, 13,911 feet, and The Notch ridge. Take the Chasm Lake trail west and cross the creek south to the grassy gully. Go up the gully to the cliffs and over them via a diagonal ledge to The Loft, 13,500 feet. Hike west on The Loft about one-half mile to a cairn-marked route which leads to the lower cliffs of the Palisades. A steep hundred foot descent will put you into the lower portions of the Home Stretch gully. Ascend north in the gully and admire the impressive ramparts of the Palisades as you proceed to the summit. A descent using the Keyhole route is recommended.

Mount Evans

14,264

From the Top: The only paved road above 14,000 feet in the country automatically makes this summit unique. Longs Peak to the north is easily visible due to its block-like top. Pikes Peak can be seen SSE. But the best view has to be of Denver at night with its millions of stationary and moving lights.

Grand Slam: 14
54 Highest: 12

Mount Bierstadt

14,060

From the Top: The twin summits of Grays and Torreys help to define the Continental Divide to the west. Further left, if there is still snow on the high peaks, the namesake snowfield of Holy Cross can be seen on the western horizon. Keep turning to see the vast expanse of South Park. Perhaps you can spot cars moving on US-285, as it crosses Kenosha Pass into South Park.

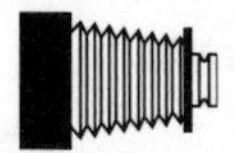

Grand Slam: 10, 15, 16-17
54 Highest: 12

Guanella Pass

From downtown Georgetown drive south on Clear Creek County 381, 11 miles to Guanella Pass, 11,669 feet. Look east from the pass to survey the route. The key to any Guanella Pass route is the willows surrounding Scott Gomer Creek. They may look like gentle knee high shrubs from the pass, but they're 10 foot high 'man eaters' so beware.

Spot the large tarn NE of the pass. Hike to its south shore and pick up a trail heading east. Once past the tarn the willows are manageable.

Guanella Pass (Evans) ■

Elevation Gain: **2900 feet** Distance: **8 miles**

Turn NE after the tarn and bushwhack across a grassy wet meadow to the spruce-covered hillside. Continue SE through the spruce to a gully, Scott Gomer Creek, which leads to the grassy west slopes of Mount Spalding. Use the cliffs that lead into the Sawtooth as a guide and stay north of them as you continue east. It's a long ridge walk east to the summit(s) of Evans.

Guanella Pass (Bierstadt) ●

Elevation Gain: **2600 feet** Distance: **6 miles**

After the tarn a good trail leads SE through more willows for a mile, then it's open tundra to Bierstadt's SW ridge. Follow the SW ridge the remaining few hundred feet to the summit.

Sawtooth (Evans–Bierstadt) ◆

Elevation Gain: **1200 feet** Distance: **.5 mile**

The Sawtooth is not particularly difficult, if you're

on the correct route. Just as good is the parallel route between Abyss Lake, 12,650 feet, and The Sawtooth ridge.

From Bierstadt: drop NE from the summit staying just east of The Sawtooth ridge. Go down until it's almost flat and decide, either cut west back to the ridge for The Sawtooth or continue NE to gain Evans' high rocky west ridge. If you decided on The Sawtooth, the trail follows a set of ledges along the west side of the ridge. In less than an hour the cairn-marked trail will lead to the grassy west slope of Evans-Spalding.

From Evans: look for a cairn-marked route leading down the grassy west slopes along the cliffs. Follow the ledges down and south, when you get to the low point, the first opening to the east, of The Sawtooth ridge it is easiest to drop down the hundred feet rather than fight the steep ridge up to Bierstadt. Then, staying east of the ridge, go up a steep rocky slope to Bierstadt.

Summit Lake (Evans) ●

Elevation Gain: **1400 feet** Distance: **4 miles**

Any number of routes are possible from Summit Lake, 12,830 feet. The easiest would be to hike to the east ridge and follow it to the summit. Another possibility is by going west over Mount Spalding, 13,842 feet, and then following Evans' west ridge to the summit.

Grays Peak

14,270

From the Top: The top of the Continental Divide in America makes for an unbroken panorama of mountains. To the southwest are several ski areas; Keystone and Breckenridge are most easily spotted.

South of Breckenridge is the fluted north slope of Quandary. From Quandary the nearby triple of Lincoln, Democrat and Bross should be evident.

Grand Slam: 18, 19
54 Highest: 16-17

Torreys Peak

14,267

From the Top: To the north and down 4000 feet is I-70 and the Bakerville Bridge. With binoculars you can see cars on US-6 as it winds up to Loveland Pass. Holy Cross is visible on the western horizon.

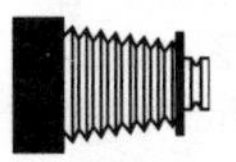

Grand Slam: 18, 19
54 Highest: 16-17

Stevens Gulch ●

Elevation Gain: **3700 feet** Distance: **6 miles**

At mile marker 221 on Interstate 70 turn off at Bakerville, and drive south on a steep dirt road for 3.1 miles to the trailhead, 11,200 feet, just before Stevens Mine.

Cross the creek and hike SW 3 miles up a very good trail to the summit of Grays. At about 13,200 feet, as the trail nears the cliffs to the east, mountain goats are often seen. With patience they are easily approached and very curious. From the summit descend north to the saddle, 13,700 feet, with Torreys and continue along the gentle ridge to the top. Descend back to the saddle and pick up a cutoff trail heading east under Grays summit to rejoin the main trail. This cutoff can be used to ascend Torreys first or by itself.

Chihuahua Gulch ●

Elevation Gain: **4500 feet** Distance: **8 miles**

Starting at Keystone on US-6 look for the Montezuma turnoff heading south. Follow the Snake River 4.7 miles and look for a galvanized guard rail on the left.

Turn behind the guard rail onto the Peru Creek Road. Follow this rocky road 2.2 miles east to a sometime marked turnoff, 10,421 feet, for Chihuahua Gulch. This 4WD road is very rough and leads in 2 miles to the trailhead at 11,200 feet.

Hike north to the saddle, 12,560 feet, between Grizzly and Torreys then follow the Continental Divide east to the summit. Descend south along the ridge to Grays. Return by heading down Grays' SW ridge and either bear south to a small mine and road in Ruby Gulch or stay on the ridge to Chihuahua Gulch.

Horseshoe Basin (Grays) ●

Elevation Gain: **2500 feet** Distance: **4.2 miles**

Continue east on the Peru Creek road 4 miles past Chihuahua Gulch to the end of the road high, 12,000 feet, in Horseshoe Basin.

Hike west to Grays south ridge and continue north along the ridge to the summit.

Grizzly Gulch (Torreys) ■

Elevation Gain: **3500 feet** Distance: **5 miles**

At mile marker 221 on Interstate 70 turn off at Bakerville, and drive south on a steep gravel road 1.1 miles to the right fork for Grizzly Gulch. Continue another mile until the road ends, 10,800 feet.

Hike 2 miles SW until you break timberline, then cut south up the steep NE ridge of Torreys to the summit.

Pikes Peak

14,110

From the Top: It is possible to see Pikes Peak from the Colorado-Wyoming border 150 miles to the north, and the view from the summit seems limitless. To the west the high summits of the Sangre de Cristo and Sawatch Ranges can be identified by the practiced eye. Take a map and see how many you can locate.

Grand Slam: 20, 21
54 Highest: 15

Barr Trail ●

Elevation Gain: **7200 feet** Distance: **23 miles**

From US-24 turn south onto Manitou Avenue and follow it less than two miles into downtown Manitou Springs. Turn left onto Ruxton until just past the cog railway depot. The Barr Trail parking lot, 6,900 feet, is up a steep road to the right.

Hike up a series of switchbacks and follow the trail up and west to gain the ridge. Continue west on this trail for almost 12 miles to the summit. As a measure of your progress, the Barr Camp shelter, 10,000 feet, is 5 miles up the trail. A possible remedy for this long route is to draw straws with a friend and have the loser drive to the summit so the winner can avoid a long descent. It may be possible to ride the cog railroad down—inquire.

Quandary Peak

14,265

From the Top: The northern summits of the Sawatch Range from La Plata to Holy Cross form a western arc. South Park can be viewed looking over Hoosier Pass. Many mines dot the slopes of North Star Mountain, slightly more than a mile south. See if you can follow the imaginary line of the Continental Divide as it goes from Hoosier Pass, then west over North Star Mountain to Fremont and Tennessee Passes before disappearing between Massive and Holy Cross.

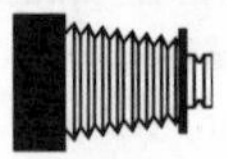

Grand Slam: 25
54 Highest: 18

Monte Cristo Creek ●

Elevation Gain: **3300 feet** Distance: **5.5 miles**

From Breckenridge drive south on CO-9, 7 miles, to Monte Cristo Creek. Drive west one-half mile to an old mine road heading NE up the open timber slopes and park, 11,000 feet.

Hike NE up the mine road to the wide ridge and turn west. Follow the ridge west through open timber, past timberline to the summit.

Blue Lakes ■

Elevation Gain: **2600 feet** Distance: **2 miles**

From CO-9 it is 2.5 miles west along Monte Cristo Creek to Blue Lakes, 11,748 feet. Park just below the dam.

Look for a steep grassy slope just west of the dam and climb directly to the summit of Quandary. A steep snow gully which parallels this route offers a fast glissade down. Beware, steep snow is potentially hazardous.

Mosquito Range

Mount Lincoln

14,286

From the Top: Colorado's eighth highest summit has mine structures encircling its high top. Most of them are but flattened kindling piles today, nonetheless a testament to the determination of our forefathers. Many distant summits are visible and with careful attention naming them will not be too difficult from this oxygen-starved pinnacle.

Grand Slam: 26
54 Highest: 22-23

Mount Bross

14,172

From the Top: Bross has the best view of the immense South Park. Sherman is but eight miles south and still it is hard to locate due to several Century summits surrounding its flanks.

Grand Slam: 27
54 Highest: 22-23

Mount Democrat

14,148

From the Top: The extensive Climax Mine just below and north of Democrat is a sobering realization of our demand for metal and the price the earth must pay. Easily the largest surface mine in Colorado, it has already consumed one mountain summit. The tailings from this mine have long since devoured the town of Kokomo, north of Fremont Pass.

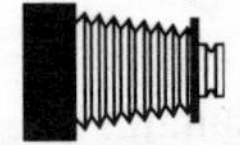

Grand Slam: 22, 26
54 Highest: 22-23

Kite Lake ●

Elevation Gain: **3500 feet** Distance: **7 miles**

From downtown Alma drive west on Park County 8, along Buckskin Creek, 6 miles, to Kite Lake, 12,033 feet. Park County 8 is seldom marked and is best located by being directly across from the Texaco sign along CO-9. This road will be blocked by snow early in the year and may require 4WD the last mile.

From the lake hike north to the saddle, 13,400 feet, between Cameron and Democrat. Follow the trail from the saddle up Democrat's east face to the flat area, 14,000 feet, and continue to the summit. An old cabin can still be seen on this flat area. Descend back to the saddle and continue east, skirting Cameron on a good trail north of its summit. At about 14,000 Lincoln will be visible 3/4 of a mile east. A slight drop and then a long flat walk will put you on Lincoln. Return to the flat area and this time skirt Cameron on the SE for the long and easy traverse to Bross. From Bross descend west to Kite Lake. Look for the fields of small scree which makes the descent such a joy.

Windy Ridge (Bross) ●

Elevation Gain: **2200 feet** Distance: **5 miles**

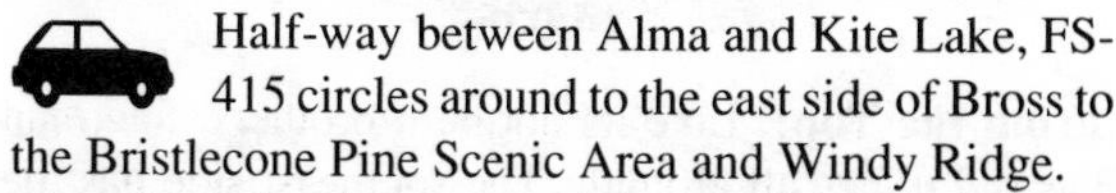

Half-way between Alma and Kite Lake, FS-415 circles around to the east side of Bross to the Bristlecone Pine Scenic Area and Windy Ridge.

From the scenic area continue generally NW on a 4WD road to the summit of Bross. A number of sub-roads fork off of this road to provide the only route challenge. Also many mine buildings and adits, horizontal mine shafts, exist along the road.

Quartzville Creek (Lincoln) ●

Elevation Gain: **2400 feet** Distance: **7.5 miles**

Starting at the north city limits of Alma, on CO-9, turn left on Park County 6 and follow the gravel road north. After 3.1 miles turn left onto Roberts Road. Several switch-backs and 1.6 miles later make a right turn at FS-247.

Follow 247 north and west as it passes timberline between Bross and Lincoln. At about 13,000 feet the road cuts back NE to gain Lincoln's east ridge and continues up to about 13,900 feet. A short scramble from the road's end will put you on the summit.

Mount Sherman

14,036

From the Top: Like its northern brothers, Sherman has old mines all around. The southeast side has the Dauntless and Hilltop mines. To the west is the Continental Chief directly below the summit. Further west are Leadville, Turquoise Reservoir and Mount Massive.

Grand Slam: 28, 29
54 Highest: 20

Fourmile Creek ●

Elevation Gain: **2000 feet** Distance: **5 miles**

From US-285 and CO-9, Fairplay, drive south on 285 1.2 miles to Park County 18 and turn west. Follow 18, 1.1 miles west to a fork, take the left fork, FS-421, 8.4 miles to the old mill, 11,700 feet. Most of the road to the mill is an old railroad grade. Past the mill remnants of the aerial tram between the Hilltop Mine and mill are visible. Continue NW 2 miles to timberline where the road is barricaded just before the Dauntless Mine, 12,300 feet.

Hike up the road toward the Hilltop Mine, 12,900 feet, high above. Follow the road around to the right and circle back above the Hilltop. Continue NW to the saddle, 13,140 feet, between Sherman and Sheridan. Then hike NNE along the ridge to the summit.

Iowa Gulch ●

Elevation Gain: **2100 feet** Distance: **3.5 miles**

From the south end of Leadville's main street, Harrison, turn east on E Monroe. Go 2-3 blocks until a tee and turn right on Toledo, Lake County 2. Follow Lake County 2 for 4 miles on a paved road to where a a gravel fork bears left, just before the ASARCO mine. Take the gravel fork 3 miles to a barricade, 12,000 feet, at the Continental Chief Mine. Two choices exist for the summit:

1. Hike north up the road and continue to the saddle between Dyer and Gemini, then follow the ridge east over Gemini to gain Sherman from the north. The Dyer–Gemini ridge has some cliffs close to Gemini so it is best to gain the saddle just east of the prominent power line.

2. Drop down and cross Iowa Creek and contour SE to the saddle between Sherman and Sheridan. From the saddle continue NNE to the summit. Both choices can be combining for a circle route.

Mosquito Pass ■

Elevation Gain: **1900 feet** Distance: **10 miles**

From Mosquito Pass, 13,185 feet, or the antenna farm south on the ridge, hike south to the summit of Mount Evans, 13,577 feet. From the summit cairn most of the route is visible in a 45 degree arc south and east. The visible features left to right are Gemini Peak, 13,951 feet, Mount Sherman, and Dyer Mountain, 13,855 feet. Head south from Evans for the connecting ridge to Dyer. This short, thin ridge is 15 minutes of cautious steep rock which will deposit you on the grassy NE slopes of Dyer. Contour SE to the saddle between Dyer and Gemini. It is easiest to lose some elevation here to avoid loose large rock that a straight approach would dictate. From the saddle stay on the tight ridge rock and head for the gully between Gemini's twin summits. Once in the saddle between Gemini's summits turn south less than a mile to the summit of Sherman. Slight detours from this route will put you on two Century summits in addition to Sherman.

Westcliffe to South Colony Lakes

Elevation Gain: **3400 feet** Distance: **7 miles**

From Westcliffe, follow CO-69 south 4.5 miles and turn right on Colfax Lane. Travel south on Colfax 4.5 miles until a tee intersection.

Turn right at the tee and head west. The gravel road rapidly gets steeper and rougher as it climbs the glacial moraine. From the tee it's 6.5 miles to the end of the road, 11,400 feet, at the base of Broken Hand Peak.

Lower South Colony Lake, 11,700 feet, is less than a mile north of the road. About one-half mile before the end of the road, another marked trail follows the creek to the lake.

Humboldt Peak

14,064

From the Top: East of Humboldt is the broad Wet Mountain Valley with the twin towns of Westcliffe and Silver Cliff as its economic hub. Far more imposing are the eastern faces of Crestone Needle and Crestone Peak as they rise precipitously out of South Colony Valley. North of the Crestones is the Bears Playground and Kit Carson Mountain.

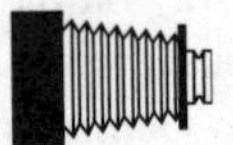

Grand Slam: 33
54 Highest: 53

South Colony Lakes ■

Elevation Gain: **2400 feet** Distance: **3 miles**

From Lower South Colony Lake stay east of the lake on a good trail to the upper lake. Look for a cairn-marked trail going steeply east and then north to Humboldt's west saddle, 12,850 feet. Follow the ridge east to the flat top just below 14,000 feet. Continue one-half mile east to the summit.

Kit Carson Mountain

14,165

From the Top: To the north is the steep north face of Kit Carson with the grassy expanse of Willow Creek beyond. South is the north face of Crestone Peak with the continuation of the red gully and its distinct cliff as the gully bends west. The hundred-mile-long San Luis Valley dominates the western view with the distant San Juans on the horizon.

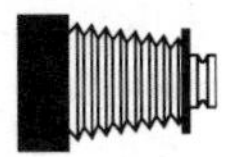

Grand Slam: 30, 34-35, 112
54 Highest: 52

South Colony Lakes ♦♦

Elevation Gain: **2900 feet** Distance: **5.5 miles**

From Lower South Colony Lake stay east of the lake on a good trail to the upper lake. Look for a cairn-marked trail going steeply east and then north to Humboldt's west saddle, 12,850 feet. Follow the ridge west going over the crest, 13,290 feet, to the Bears Playground, 13,140 feet. Diagonal across the Bears Playground skirting south of the 13,799 foot unnamed summit to a broad SE facing gully on the 13,900 foot east summit. The broad and solid SE gully quickly leads to the east summit. Once on the east summit, Kit Carson is very visible but not the route. The east summit has a crescent shaped flat top about 100 feet long. Descend down a 50 foot wide gully about in the middle of the crescent. This gully drops about 300 feet into a south facing gravel gully about 100 feet below the main ridge. Cross the south gravel gully and head up the next gully NW back to the ridge for the final ascent. Return to the Bears Playground and when you reach the headwall above the lakes descend your favorite steep chute into the basin and pick your way down.

Spanish Creek ◆

Elevation Gain: **5900 feet** Distance: **10 miles**

Just south of Moffat on CO-17 turn east toward the town of Crestone. Travel 12 miles east until about a mile west of Crestone at the Baca Grande subdivision, turn south. Drive SE on El Camino Real following an old railroad grade past Willow Creek and stop at Spanish Creek, 8300 feet.

Hike east following Spanish Creek on a faint trail until just above timberline and even with Kit Carson's magnificent SW ships prow. Climb to the summit via the gully between the ships prow and the 13,900 foot east summit. This route avoids the steep descent from the east summit and is very uncrowded as a bonus.

Crestone Peak

14,294

From the Top: Kit Carson to the north looks like a faceted jewel with its many glacier-carved ridges. Southward along the western foothills of the Sangre de Cristo are the immense sand dunes of Sand Dunes National Monument. Just beyond is the Sierra Blanca with its four fourteeners.

Grand Slam: 34-35, 37
54 Highest: 55, 56-57

South Colony Lakes ♦♦

Elevation Gain: **2700 feet** Distance: **6 miles**

From Lower South Colony Lake stay east of the lake on a good trail to the upper lake. Look for a cairn-marked trail going steeply east and then north to Humboldt's west saddle, 12,850 feet. Follow the ridge west going over the crest, 13,290 feet, to the Bears Playground, 13,140 feet. Circle south above the headwall to the north face of Crestone Peak. Look for a rock ledge catwalk which leads to the base of Crestone's red gully. Carefully cross the ice to the west side of the gully and make your way up the steep rock to the saddle, 14,170 feet, between the twin summits of Crestone Peak. The west summit is slightly higher and is a moderate ridge walk from the saddle.

Crestone Needle

14,197

From the Top: The small summit looks directly down onto Colony Lakes, 2500 feet below. To the northwest are the summits of Crestone and Kit Carson. Notice the steep ridge connecting the two Crestones. Pikes Peak can be seen on the northeast horizon.

Grand Slam: FC, 34-35, 36, 37
54 Highest: 6, 54, 56-57, BC

South Colony Lakes ♦♦

Elevation Gain: **2500 feet** Distance: **4 miles**

From Lower South Colony Lake circle around the south side of the lake past the willows and head up the very steep grassy gully, to the saddle, 12,900 feet, between Broken Hand and the Needle. From the saddle follow a grassy trail north to the steep south ridge. The object is to reach the left most of three gullies by going up and west. Each of the two ridges which have to be crossed present their own challenges. The third gully is long, straight, steep and not exposed. It joins the summit ridge about one hundred yards south for a short walk to the top.

Needle to Peak

Several possibilities exist to ascend Crestone Peak from Crestone Needle.

Go south to Cottonwood Lake ◆

Return via the ascent route to the grassy ridge between Broken Hand and Crestone Needle. Make your way SW to Cottonwood Lake and follow the Cottonwood Lake route to Crestone Peak.

Go north to the first ridge saddle ◆◆

1. Rappel north on the ridge to the first saddle, with a great view of the South Colony Lakes between your legs.

2. Descend north and find a steep rocky gully heading west which stops at a 70 degree cliff about 50 feet above and west of the first saddle. Free climb to the saddle making use of numerous great hand and foot holds.

From the first ridge saddle two more choices:

1. Descend west about 1000 feet to avoid numerous steep cliffs and then head north up the red gully to the saddle, 14,170 feet, between the east and west summits of Crestone Peak.

2. Instead of descending, skirt the major pinnacles on the west and stay on the ridge to the east summit, very difficult and exposed.

Crestone Peak to South Colony Lakes

◆ 1. Descend south to Cottonwood Lake and gain the 600 feet back to the Broken Hand saddle.

◆◆ 2. At the red saddle descend on the steep and often

icy north side about 1000 feet to a high exit heading NE. This exit is very important because of cliffs further down the red gully. Follow a series of ledges NE to the Bears Playground. When you reach the headwall above the lakes, pick your favorite steep chute into the basin.

Cottonwood Lake (Needle & Peak) ◆

Elevation Gain: **5900 feet** Distance: **9.5 miles**

From Moffat on CO-17 travel 12 miles east on a paved road toward the town of Crestone. About a mile west of Crestone is the Baca Grande subdivision, turn south. Drive SE on El Camino Real following an old railroad grade, crossing first Willow Creek, Spanish Creek and stopping at the Cottonwood Creek water tank, 8400 feet.

Hike NE following the creek on a decent trail until a major fork. Follow the left fork north to Cottonwood Lake, 12,310 feet, and camp.

The Needle and the Peak can be two separate climbs from Cottonwood Lake. For Crestone Needle, climb the grassy slope NE to the saddle between Broken Hand and the Needle and use the South Colony Lake route description. For Crestone Peak, skirt the Needle's SW buttress and head north for the red gully. This gully goes to the saddle, 14,170 feet, between the two summits. Although the west summit is a few feet higher, both are worth the effort for their respective views.

Mount Lindsey

14,042

From the Top: Eastward is La Veta Pass with the impressive bulk of West Spanish Peak, 13,626 feet, slightly south. From the pass and south of the summit in a large sweep are the Forbes Ranch properties. Lindsey's summit is on private land. To the west is Blanca and a number of high alpine basins with inviting lakes. An unnamed Century summit is less than a mile northeast of the Iron Nipple.

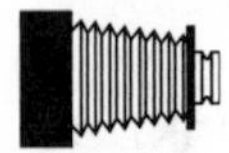

Grand Slam: 39
54 Highest: 58

Huerfano Basin ■

Elevation Gain: **3500 feet** Distance: **7.5 miles**

If traveling south on I-25 turn west at Exit 56, Red Rock Road, this saves about 10 miles compared to going into Walsenburg. Red Rock Road connects to CO-69 in less than 5 miles of good gravel. Continue NW to Gardner and follow CO-69 west one-half mile to the Red Wing Road and turn west. Travel west 7 miles until a fork and stay right. Another 5 miles and another fork at a small white boxy aluminum sided building, take the left fork paralleling the Huerfano River. The left fork follows the river for 8 miles to the San Isabel NF boundary. Continue 2.2 miles further to the trailhead at 10,600 feet. Almost the entire road to the trailhead can be traveled by a high clearance 2WD vehicle.

From the trailhead, survey the route to the south and east. Directly south is the impressive north face of Blanca and as you scan left, part of the connecting ridge to Lindsey is visible. Further left is an imposing ridge with a steep box canyon to its east. Above this ridge is the Iron Nipple. Your route is to the right of this ridge up a steep timbered slope.

Hike south through alternate open meadows and heavy timber following the old road. After a long mile the road will end at the river–you missed the right turn back a hundred yards. Either backtrack or stay west of the river as you continue south for a couple hundred yards. The trail will reappear in a large wet meadow.

Staying close to the river, look for two things: one a river crossing and two a gully leading high and SE in dense timber. Cross the river and follow a steep foot path parallel to a large creek and head toward the Iron Nipple, 13,500 feet, some bushwhacking is required. After the steep, dense timber is a beautiful grassy sloped mass of tundra with the tip of Lindsey looming larger to the SE. Contour west and south around the Iron Nipple to its connecting ridge, 13,150 feet, with Lindsey.

To gain the summit either stay on the north ridge or contour east of the ridge for one of several steep gullies. Two Century peaks are accessible from this valley, 1) An unnamed summit, 13,828 feet, one mile NE of the Iron Nipple, and 2) California Peak, 13,849 feet, west of the trailhead.

Colorado 150 to Lake Como

Elevation Gain: **3700 feet** Distance: **5 miles**

From the intersection of US-160 and CO-150 travel north on 150 3.2 miles and turn east crossing a cattle guard. A dirt road can be seen heading NE toward the Sierra Blanca massif.

Follow the dirt road along a fence line and then up and rough to Lake Como, 6 miles. Most 2WD vehicles can make the first 2 miles, 90 percent of 4WD's quit before reaching Holbrook Creek at 5 miles. If your vehicle makes it to Lake Como it's possible to go as far as Blue Lakes. This is a very rough road with large loose cobbles and steep grades. The end of the 2WD portion is at 8000 feet and the road crosses Holbrook Creek at 10,700 feet. That's 2700 feet in 3 miles for an average grade of 17 percent. After the creek the road gets rougher and steeper.

A good place to park is at the ghost town of Commodore, several hundred yards before Holbrook Creek. You will recognize it because of the half-dozen foundations and collapsed buildings along the road. There is good camping east of Lake Como, 11,750 feet, and up further around Blue Lakes, 12,100 feet.

Ellingwood Point

14,042

From the Top: The north face of Blanca dominates the southern horizon. Slightly west is Little Bear with the connecting ridge between them. Northeast is the Huerfano River Basin with Lily Lake just below the summit. Lake Como can be seen at the edge of the trees to the west.

Grand Slam: 38
54 Highest: 59

Blanca Peak

14,345

From the Top: Located at the corner of three counties, Huerfano, Costilla, and Alamosa, you have a measure of the importance of this summit. To the south, west and north lies a patchwork quilt of farms in the vast San Luis Valley. Closer, you can look down on the famed Blanca-Little Bear Ridge. To the north are the Crestones with numerous summits in between.

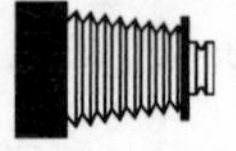

Grand Slam: 6, 38
54 Highest: 50

Lake Como ■

Elevation Gain: **3000 feet** Distance: **5 miles**

Both summits are visible from Lake Como but hard to discern because of their position high up the basin. Hike up the basin NE, passing north of Crater Lake, 12,700 feet, on the north. Continue NE to the saddle between Blanca and Ellingwood at 13,700 feet. Follow the ridge south to Blanca's summit. Ellingwood is NW but the ridge is too steep so contour along the SW side and regain the ridge half-way to the summit. Do not attempt to descend SW from Ellingwood rather return to the saddle trail.

Little Bear Peak

14,037

From the Top: A series of steep ridges emanate from Little Bear's summit. As they disappear the next thing one sees is the agricultural patchwork miles below. The ridge to the east connects to Blanca and is very rugged.

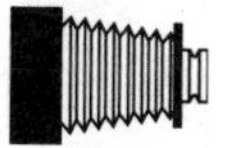

Grand Slam: 40, 41
54 Highest: 61

Lake Como ♦♦

Elevation Gain: **2300 feet** Distance: **3 miles**

About halfway between Lake Como and Blue Lakes a distinct notch in the ridge to the south is visible. Climb to this notch via the steep loose gully, taking care not to roll rocks on fellow climbers. From the notch, 12,600 feet, go east either on top of or slightly south of the ridge until it becomes too steep. Contour south of Little Bear's west buttress to where the south and west ridges form a vee. If dry go directly up this very steep vee to a series of short gullies to the summit. If snow-covered stay left and work your way up even steeper rock to the short gullies. Hard hats are in order due to the abundance of loose rock. Most people rappel down this steep section using one of several fixed anchors. A free climb works equally well—very manly.

Little Bear—Blanca—Ellingwood ♦♦

The best route for all three is first Little Bear and then the connecting ridge to Blanca, allow 3 hours. Once on the ridge you must go to either Blanca or Little Bear because their are no intermediate descents. If the weather is still favorable then 1 hour will have you on and off Ellingwood. Another argument for this route is that it's easier to ascend rather than descend steep rock. Technical knowledge is a must for the ridge, ropes are optional. Good Luck!!!

Culebra Range

Culebra Peak

14,047

From the Top: The view west is blocked by the high west ridge. Northeast are the twin summits of the Spanish Peaks. Below and east is the small locale of Torres. To the south is a Century peak, Red Mountain, 13,908 feet.

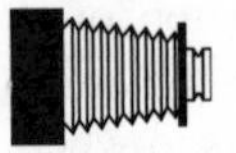

Grand Slam: 42
54 Highest: 60

Taylor Ranch ●

Elevation Gain: **5000 feet** Distance: **16 miles**
Season: Memorial Day–Labor Day
Cost: $25 per person
Ranch foreman: Jim Cockrum, 719-672-3580

The Taylor Ranch allows climbing any day between Memorial and Labor Days. You must call ahead to have someone meet you at the locked gate. San Luis is a good choice for this, do not count on Chama having a pay phone. You will be required to sign a liability waiver. The ranch may allow access via 4WD vehicles—inquire.

From San Luis turn east on 4th Street, between the Phillips 66 and Texaco stations. This may also be marked as CO-142. Drive SE about 4 miles to Chama and a road marked L.7. The Taylor ranch gate is 4 miles east of Chama on the south side of Culebra Creek. Several bridges cross Culebra Creek to a road marked M.5. Follow M.5 east until it dead ends at the locked Taylor Ranch gate. From the gate it's about a mile to the main ranch buildings.

From the ranch buildings, 9,000 feet, hike east along the road and immediately take the right fork. Follow this road through the aspen 4 miles to 4-Way, an old road crossing at 11,200 feet. Continue at constant elevation along the south side of the ridge another mile until the road meets a small creek. Follow this creek east gaining the cairn-marked ridge, 13,330 feet. Hike south along the ridge and then SE to Culebra's west false summit, 13,920 feet. Continue SE another half-mile to the summit.

Mount of the Holy Cross

14,005

From the Top: The view from the top is one of geologically recent glaciation. Steeply sculpted U-shaped valleys with bare rock walls make it unlike any other Sawatch fourteener. Looking south the monarches of the Sawatch, Elbert and Massive are quickly spotted. Torreys and Grays on the divide far to the east are easy to identify.

Grand Slam: 46(2)
54 Highest: 39

Half Moon Pass ■

Elevation Gain: **4500 feet** Distance: **9.5 miles**

From Interstate 70 and US-24 travel 4 miles south to Forest Service 707. FS-707 follows the west side of the Eagle River just where US-24 crosses to the east side of the river. Follow 707 for 5 twisty miles until it dead-ends at Half Moon Campground and trailhead, 10,400 feet.

Hike west to Half Moon Pass, 11,600 feet, and descend to where the trail spans East Cross Creek, 10,700 feet. Then head SW through tall timber to the north ridge of Holy Cross. Follow this ridge until it meets the north face and then turn east for the last 500 feet to the summit. This is among the most scenic fourteeners in Colorado starting from Half Moon Pass to the summit.

Mount Massive

14,421

From the Top: The most distinctive view from Massive is not even in the Sawatch Range, but rather in the nearby Elk Mountains. Mount Sopris, not even 13,000 feet, stands as a lone sentinel at the northwest corner of the Elks. The reason such a relatively low mountain stands out is its almost 7000 feet of relief compared to the nearby Crystal River Valley. To the east Leadville commands the high ground of the broad upper Arkansas Valley.

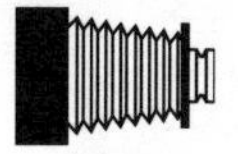

Grand Slam: 49
54 Highest: 34

Colorado Trail ●

Elevation Gain: **4400 feet** Distance: **11 miles**

From Leadville drive 3 miles west on US-24 to where 24 turns south and turn right on CO-300. Drive west on 300 .8 mile and turn left on Lake County 11, Halfmoon Road. Follow 11 south 1.5 miles where it turns sharply right. It's 6 more miles to the spot where the Colorado Trail crosses Halfmoon Creek, 10,064 feet. A small trailhead parking lot, usually filled by 8AM, is just north of the creek.

Hike north on the Colorado Trail for 3 miles to where it intersects the Mount Massive trail, 11,200 feet. Follow the Mount Massive trail NW for a mile, quickly passing timberline. Continue west to the saddle between Massive and its southern 14,000 foot summit. This saddle is 13,900 leaving the last 500 feet along a rocky ridge, the best part of the trip! A free form descent is possible because of Massive's soft contours. Be sure to hit the trail before timberline to avoid bushwhacking through dense timber.

North Halfmoon Creek ■

Elevation Gain: **3900 feet** Distance: **5.5 miles**

Drive west 2.5 miles past the Colorado Trail to the bridge, 10,500 feet, over Halfmoon Creek and park.

Follow the trail north along the east side of Halfmoon Creek for 2 miles. A large cairn marks the turnoff for the grunt ahead. The next 3,000 feet to the saddle between Massive and its south summit will test legs and lungs. This route is shorter and steeper than the Colorado Trail. The reward is one-tenth the number of fellow climbers.

Mount Elbert

14,433

From the Top: A 360 degree panorama of fourteeners can be seen from Colorado's highest. North are Massive and Holy Cross, east is Sherman, south are all the summits of the Sawatch, and west is Snowmass with its expansive namesake snowfield still visible in early summer.

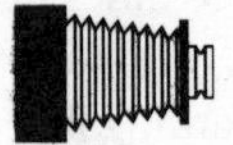

Grand Slam: 44, 50, 51
54 Highest: 38

Colorado Trail ●

Elevation Gain: **4400 feet** Distance: **6.5 miles**

Starting at the junction of the Colorado Trail and Halfmoon Creek Road, 10,064 feet (see Mount Massive) is the beginning of the most popular route up Elbert. Hike south on the Colorado Trail for less than 2 miles until a spur heads SW along the NE rib of Elbert. As a measure of your progress you will break timberline just below 12,000 feet, only 2,500 to go.

South Halfmoon Creek ■

Elevation Gain: **4000 feet** Distance: **9 miles**

Continue driving west 2 miles past the Colorado Trail and look for a road that fords Halfmoon Creek. The road will be slightly west of where the south fork joins Halfmoon Creek. This is a major league 4WD road that takes you to timberline between French and Elbert.

Steep grassy routes exist to the south or pick one of many steeper gullies to the summit. French Peak, 13,922 feet, is a Century peak along with several others in the area.

Mount Elbert Trail ●

Elevation Gain: **4300 feet** Distance: **8.5 miles**

Starting from CO-82 about 1/4 mile east of the Twin Lakes visitor center, follow a paved road, Lake County 24, 1.3 miles NW as it climbs a lateral moraine. When the paved road forks at right-hand U-turn, turn-off to the left. The left paved fork immediately dead-ends and a dirt road turns left from the pavement.

Following the paved road to the east side of the pumped storage reservoir will get you an excellent view of the terrain to the summit.

Follow the dirt road, easy 4WD when dry, 2-3 miles to several small man-made ponds and a cabin, 10,250 feet.

Just west of the ponds is a faint trail through the aspen which goes to the summit. If the trail turns into a faint road heading past timberline, congratulations you've found the correct trail. This "road" was used just after WWII to get an army Jeep to the summit. Overall the trail is quite good, just faint, at the start and non-existent past 13,000.

Bull Hill ■

Elevation Gain: **5300 feet** Distance: **9 miles**

If you can find the trailhead, 10,000 feet, this is an excellent alternative to the busy eastern approaches for Elbert. The trailhead is less than 1/4 mile off of CO-82 at the entrance to Echo Canyon. Start looking 1.8 miles west of the Mt. Elbert Lodge, Bed & Breakfast. The turnoff is .5 mile west of mile marker 73 on CO-82. This seldom marked canyon road appears to start in the front yard of a cabin and then swings to the west and north for a quarter-mile into dense aspen. If you find a massive concrete foundation, an old tram, you're there.

Hike east across Echo creek, just below the foundation, following the old mine road. The trail will switch back and forth on the south side of Bull Hill until 12,500 feet. Caution, do not follow the Echo Creek trail. Proceed to just east of Bull Hill's summit, 13,773 feet, and follow the connecting ridge NNE to Elbert, the saddle's low point is about 13,250 feet. For those of us who are high altitude junkies this route keeps you above 13000 for hours, i.e. not the best for "Monsoon Season." A great view of this route can be had from La Plata Peak and also 2 miles up the South Fork of Lake Creek Road.

La Plata Peak

14,336

From the Top: On the western horizon five of the Elk fourteeners can be identified: from left to right look for Castle, Maroon, Pyramid, Snowmass and Capitol. Closer on the Continental Divide, between Pyramid and Snowmass, is Grizzly Peak, 13,988 feet, thought to be a fourteener until a re-survey in the late 1940's.

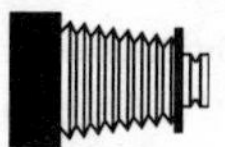

Grand Slam: 52, 53
54 Highest: 8-9, 30

South Fork ■

Elevation Gain: **4200 feet** Distance: **7 miles**

Cross Lake Creek at the South Fork bridge, 10,200 feet, along CO-82 and park along the road south of the bridge.

Follow the trail east along Lake Creek until it comes to the South Fork of Lake Creek. Look for a foot bridge to the east side of the creek and cross. Continue east to La Plata Gulch Creek and hike south up the gulch and then angle up through the timber to the ridge separating La Plata Basin from La Plata Gulch. The fine north face of La Plata is now visible. Follow the ridge to the summit, staying west of the north face.

Winfield ●

Elevation Gain: **4200 feet** Distance: **6 miles**

Winfield is 12 miles west of US-24 on a good graded road, Chaffee County 390. If you can find the trailhead, no small task, this gets my vote as the finest climb in the Sawatch.

4WD west on a rough but not steep road 1.8 miles from downtown Winfield, going past the cemetery and crossing several streams. Look for a faint road branching right at an inclined meadow. This road heads north through the aspens for several hundred yards and is barricaded by a large tubular steel gate.

Do not follow the road anymore, rather hike along the creek just west of the gate. You will shortly be rewarded with a faint but decent trail which will lead you rapidly to a large, unnamed willow basin, the highlight of the trip. There are numerous tarns and a picturesque rocky stream all terminating in a semicircular headwall. The mile of Colorado to the headwall will test your summit resolve, so strong is the urge to just enjoy. The ridge above the headwall is quickly gained via one of several steep gullies. A large flat rocky expanse at 12,800 feet awaits you with fine views of Massive and Elbert. Continue NE to the summit.

Mount Oxford

14,153

From the Top: Look north to pick out US-24 in the wide, flat upper Arkansas Valley. Above the road on the horizon is Holy Cross. To the south is Harvard with the distant Mount Princeton to the left.

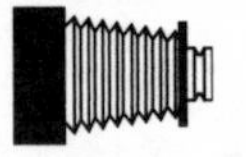

Grand Slam: 54-55, 56
54 Highest: 26-27

Mount Belford

14,197

From the Top: The rounded top of Belford offers little opportunity to examine lower features. All of the Mosquito fourteeners are within a five degree arc to the northeast.

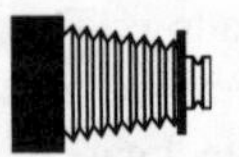

Grand Slam: 54-55, 56
54 Highest: 26-27

Missouri Mountain

14,067

From the Top: Many near and far summits can be identified from the steep summit of Missouri. Massive is directly behind Elbert and therefore obscured. Missouri Gulch lays like an open book to the north.

Grand Slam: 54-55, 57
54 Highest: 26-27

Vicksburg ■

Elevation Gain: **6900 feet** Distance: **12 miles**

The ghost town of Vicksburg, 9669 feet, is 8 miles west of US-24 along Chaffee County 390. Be sure to take in the museum on the north side of the road from the trailhead parking lot, it has many pieces of old mining memorabilia. All three summits can be done as a strenuous day hike from the trailhead, assuming Mother Nature cooperates. Fine campsites exist just above timberline along the trail to Elkhead Pass, 13,200 feet, thereby easing your time pressure.

Cross Clear Creek on a great Forest Service bridge. After a seemingly endless dose of steep switchbacks the trail heads south into Missouri Gulch. As you break out of the aspen into willow, Missouri will appear high in the valley to the right, Belford is closer and left.

Missouri

Head for the grassy slope west of the steep gullies under Missouri's summit. The summit is directly above the prominent Y-shaped gully. The grassy slope will turn to rock and get steeper as you gain the NW ridge. From the ridge it's a few hundred yards to the summit. Do not attempt the steep east ridge between the summit and Elkhead Pass. Return via the same grassy slope and staying as high as comfortable head east toward Belford.

Oxford

Either skirt Belford to the south and head straight for Oxford, or go over Belford on your way to Oxford and then return to Missouri Gulch via the south side of Belford. In either case the drop to the saddle, 13,504 feet, is easy. The former choice would have you finishing with Belford and descending via its NNW rib.

Belford

From timberline at the north edge of Missouri Gulch a trail is quite visible on Belford's NNW rib. This steep grunt leads directly to the summit.

All three summits are just as easy in either direction.

Cloyses Lake (Missouri) ●

Elevation Gain: **3100 feet** Distance: **5 miles**

From the Missouri Mountain trail sign high in the Lake Fork valley, see Huron, hike south on the trail which skirts Cloyses Lake to the east. When you see the lake, take the left trail fork SE to timberline. Gain Missouri's NW summit ridge about 1 mile from the summit by heading up the SW facing grassy slope. The summit ridge walk is a delightful view of fourteeners in a 360 degree panorama. To descend, follow the south ridge to the saddle, 13,600 feet, between Iowa Peak, 13,861 feet, and enjoy the "sugar cube sized" scree as it cushions your knees. This drainage leads directly to the trail at timberline. Do not reverse this route because of the difficulty of going up loose scree.

Huron Peak

14,005

From the Top: Even though ranked 52nd in height, Huron provides one of the best viewing summits in the Sawatch. The summit is very small with steep sides so the near view is excellent and its relative position allows for extended peak picking. My favorite is Uncompahgre eighty-plus miles to the southwest, which is characterized by its black block summit.

Grand Slam: 54-55, 58, 59
54 Highest: 24

Winfield ●

Elevation Gain: **3000 feet** Distance: **7 miles**

From Winfield, 12 miles west of US-24 on Chaffee County 390, a 4WD or hiking road heads south, crossing Clear Creek. Follow the road less than a half-mile, until it forks. Take the left fork as it switches up through the timber until a sharp U-turn at a natural saddle, 11,200 feet. From Winfield it's about 2 miles to the saddle for your choice of two routes.

1. From the saddle hike south on a closed mine road that leads around Browns' west rib and into a huge grassy basin WNW of Huron. Resist the temptation to go up the gully as the road turns to a faint trail, rather circle around and west of the prominent buttress. Following the gully will put you on Browns' west ridge with a difficult descent to the grassy basin below. Continue east in the grassy basin to just west of the saddle, then turn south to Huron's summit.

2. Stay on the jeep road to timberline, in a big bowl, NW of Browns Peak. Gain Browns' NW ridge and continue to its summit, 13,523 feet. Stay on the ridge south to the summit of Huron. Keep a sharp eye out for the goats sure to be found on the high ridges.

Cloyses Lake ■

Elevation Gain: **3000 feet** Distance: **6 miles**

On the south side of Chaffee County 390, 2 miles west of Vicksburg is a small group of cabins, Rockdale on the maps. Looking across Clear Creek, FS-381, a 4WD road, will be visible heading south on the east side of the valley. Cross Clear Creek, high water in early summer, and head south 2.4 miles to a pair of trail signs for Missouri and Huron. Another .2 mile on the road is a barbed wire fence marked private, Cloyses Lake is a few hundred yards past the fence.

From the trailhead sign follow the trail SW until you can cross Lake Fork of Clear Creek on a beaver dam, 11,000 feet. A faint trail heads through the timber to treeline. Continue west over large boulders to the saddle, 13,400 feet, between Browns and Huron. Gaining this saddle will be difficult because of steep scree and/or snow. Once on the saddle follow the "yellow brick road" south to Huron's summit.

Mount Harvard

14,420

From the Top: Look east over the much lower Mosquito Range ridge and see most of South Park, with Pikes Peak clearly visible beyond. Southward you can see a half dozen more Sawatch summits. Southwest are the San Juans with several identifiable peaks. West are the Elks with Castle closest and Capitol most distant. North are another half dozen Sawatch summits. The large lake to the west is Taylor Park Reservoir.

Grand Slam: 63
54 Highest: 36-37

Mount Columbia

14,073

From the Top: Harvard at the head of Horn Fork Basin will dominate the view from Columbia. Otherwise the Arkansas River valley from Leadville to Salida is visible. Take time to enjoy the serpentine sweep of the Continental Divide, just across Horn Fork Basin.

Grand Slam: 60-61
54 Highest: 31

Horn Fork Basin ■

Elevation Gain: **5800 feet** Distance: **13 miles**

It's 7 miles from Buena Vista to the North Cottonwood Creek trailhead. Starting at US-24 and Chaffee County 350 (Crossman Ave.), several blocks north of the stoplight, go west 2 miles. The road tees into Chaffee County 361, turn north. Follow paved 361, past where it turns to gravel, for 0.9 mile. As 361 makes a large bend to the right, a left turn will put you on Chaffee County 365. 365 dead-ends in 4 miles, of rough graded road, at the trailhead, 9900 feet.

From the trailhead follow a broad Forest Service trail west, 2 miles, to the junction with Kroenke Lake trail, hike north 3 more miles into Horn Fork Basin. When you break timberline Harvard will be visible at the north end of the basin. Columbia is to your right and defines the east wall of the basin. The easiest route has you gaining Harvard's south face just east of the south rib. A foot trail switches up the south slope to the fractured block summit of Harvard. To climb Columbia in the same day, descend east into the Frenchman Creek drainage to skirt the Harvard-Columbia ridge to the east. Descend low enough,

Fourteener C

Front Range

Longs Peak ____
Mount Evans ____
Mount Bierstadt ____
Torreys Peak ____
Grays Peak ____
Pikes Peak ____

Tenmile Range

Quandary Peak ____

Mosquito Range

Mount Lincoln ____
Mount Bross ____
Mount Democrat ____
Mount Sherman ____

Sangre de Cristo Range

Humboldt Peak ____
Kit Carson Mountain ____
Crestone Peak ____
Crestone Needle ____
Mount Lindsey ____
Ellingwood Point ____
Blanca Peak ____
Little Bear Peak ____

Culebra Range

Culebra Peak ____

Sawatc

Mount of the Holy Cross
Mount Massive
Mount Elbert
La Plata Peak
Mount Oxford
Mount Belford
Missouri Mountair
Huron Peak
Mount Harvard
Mount Columbia
Mount Yale
Mount Princeton
Mount Antero
Mount Shavano
Mount Tabeguach

Elk Mo

Castle Peak
Pyramid Peak
North Maroon Pea
Maroon Peak
Capitol Peak
Snowmass Mount

COLORADO
POCKE

imbing Log

Range

ntains

San Juans

La Garita Mountains

San Luis Peak ____________

San Juan Range

Uncompahgre Peak ____________
Wetterhorn Peak ____________
Redcloud Peak ____________
Sunshine Peak ____________
Handies Peak ____________

Sneffels Range

Mount Sneffels ____________

San Miguel Mountains

Wilson Peak ____________
Mount Wilson ____________
El Diente Peak ____________

Needle Mountains

Sunlight Peak ____________
Windom Peak ____________
Mount Eolus ____________

Grand Slam ____________

Personal Log of

____

OURTEENERS
SLAM

about 12,800 feet, to avoid the ridge and go up Columbia's grassy north slope. Descend SW from the summit back into Horn Fork Basin. Many camping possibilities exist within this basin.

Frenchman Creek / Harvard Trail ●

Elevation Gain: **5600 feet** Distance: **11 miles**

The most difficult part of this route is finding it. Starting from US-24, 7 miles north of Buena Vista, turn west on Chaffee County 386. Follow 386 as it twists and turns for 1.4 miles.

Turn left onto a faint dirt road heading west up a steep open lodgepole forest. This narrow and rocky 4WD road will parallel Frenchman Creek on a lateral moraine for about 2 miles stopping at a barricade with room for maybe 5 vehicles.

Less than a mile west on foot you cross to the south side of Frenchman Creek and shortly intersect, at 11,000 feet, the Colorado Trail and Collegiate Peak Wilderness boundary. Two miles west, the trail breaks timberline and Harvard is due west while Columbia is to the south. Both peaks tend to fade away from view inasmuch as the terrain flattens near the tops. No trails exist to either summit nor is any needed. This is a lovely, little used, high alpine valley . . . enjoy!

Mount Yale

14,196

From the Top: Yale has the best view of Horn Fork Basin with Harvard at the end and Columbia defining the eastern boundary. The Elks to the northwest line up in an almost straight line. The south boundary of the Collegiate Peaks Wilderness Area below roughly follows the Cottonwood Pass Road.

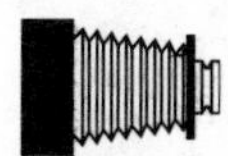

Grand Slam: 64, 65
54 Highest: 35

Denny Gulch

Starting from Buena Vista's only stoplight, U.S. 24 and Chaffee County 306, drive west 11 miles to the Collegiate Peaks Campground entrance. Several hundred yards past the entrance, at the top of the rise, but 1/2 mile before the end of the pavement is the Denny Gulch trailhead, 9847 feet. Do not confuse this with the Denny Creek trailhead at pavement's end. If you look due north, the summit of Yale is visible above the trees.

Summer ●

Elevation Gain: **4200 feet** Distance: **5 miles**

Follow Denny Gulch Creek to timberline then angle NE to the saddle between Yale and its prominent 13,440 south summit. From the saddle, 13,100 feet, follow the ridge NNW to the summit. A minor variation would be to continue along the north branch of Denny Gulch Creek to the grassy bench above timberline and ascend Yale's NW ridge. A circle route combining the two is recommended for interest and to avoid going up the loose scree to the saddle.

Winter ■

Elevation Gain: **4900 feet** Distance: **6 miles**

Because of the deep snow in the dense timber along the creek a wind-blown ridge route is best for winter. Scan the south facing slopes east of the normal trailhead looking for the driest route to timberline. Once at timberline, make mental notes for the return, and gain the ridge and travel north over the 13,440 foot south summit. Expect deep snow a couple hundred feet from Yale's summit. Winter's fewer daylight hours and the strong cold winds which keep the route snow free, make an otherwise easy climb into a much harder event.

Mount Princeton

14,197

From the Top: Because Princeton juts east from the body of the Sawatch Range, the Arkansas and Trout Creek valleys are easily viewed. Two trains once crossed Trout Creek Pass into the Arkansas Valley. One train headed north to Leadville and the other went up Chalk Creek past Saint Elmo and through the Alpine Tunnel. Both of these railroad beds can be spotted by the keen-eyed observer.

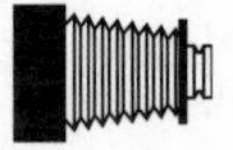

Grand Slam: 66, 67, 68-69
54 Highest: 2, 29

Frontier Ranch ●

Elevation Gain: **5200 feet** Distance: **12 miles**

Starting from Buena Vista's only stoplight, US-24 and Chaffee County 306, drive west 0.6 mile to Chaffee County 321. Follow 321 south for 7 miles and when the paved road bends to the left and a dirt road goes straight, Chaffee County 322, follow 322 for 1 mile to the Frontier Ranch.

Alternately, you can start at Nathrop, US-24 and Chaffee County 162. Travel west on 162, 4.2 miles, until just past Chalk Creek, where Chaffee County 321 joins 162 from the north. Follow 321, 1.1 miles, as it climbs the steep lateral moraine. On top of the moraine turn left onto 322 to the ranch.

A pair of magnificent entrance signs will greet you. On the left is the entrance to the ranch and the right is the Mount Princeton Trail. A large corral parking lot, 9000 feet, beckons 2WD vehicles.

At the west end of the lot a narrow 4WD road that serves as an access road goes 3 miles to the antenna farm at 10,800 feet. This road is easy to the antennas, but the remaining 1.4 miles to timberline is rough.

Just as the road breaks timberline, a trail crosses the grassy ridge on the north side and makes a broad sweep below Princeton's SE ridge. Resist the temptation to continue up the road the last half-mile to Bristlecone Park, 12,200 feet. Doing so will have you gain the 13,286 foot SE summit, up a steep slope instead of using the gentle trail. This trail leads to the faint remains of a mine. The summit will be in full view the entire way so that when the trail fades, head for the ridge and summit. There are numerous goats above timberline, so keep a sharp eye.

Mount Antero

14,269

From the Top: If the air is clear the view south over Poncha Pass shows the west side of the Sangre de Cristos as far south as the Sierra Blanca. The sand dunes are easily spotted below the Sierra Blanca. This view is best when the sun is low in the west.

Grand Slam: 67, 70, 71
54 Highest: 32-33

Baldwin Gulch ●

Elevation Gain: **4900 feet** Distance: **13 miles**

Starting from US-24 and Chaffee County 162, Nathrop, travel west on 162 12 miles to the marked turnoff, 9383 feet, for Baldwin Gulch.

Baldwin Gulch, just past the second Alpine turnoff, is a rough 4WD road and very popular with jeepers. The road crosses Baldwin Creek at 10,850 feet and continues up the west and then south sides of Antero to 13,500 feet.

Either follow the road its entire length or head straight for the summit after passing timberline. Be prepared to share the road in summer with numerous jeeps. On top of the ridge the right road fork, 13,100 feet, continues over the ridge to the SW and drops into the Browns Creek drainage, see Shavano and Tabeguache. The left fork continues east to Antero's south face, then up a series of switchbacks to a saddle, 13,500 feet. Hike north on the ridge about a mile and gain 750 feet to the summit.

Mount Shavano

14,229

From the Top: The Arkansas Valley widens considerably near Salida to the southeast and this is the commanding vantage point. Pikes Peak is a little north of east on the horizon. The San Luis Valley opens up to the south.

Grand Slam: 67, 72, 73, BC
54 Highest: 28

Mount Tabeguache

14,155

From the Top: Seven miles southwest is Monarch Pass with the antennas visible on the Continental Divide ridge and US-50 winding up the grade. Parts of Monarch Ski Area are visible. To the north the road system on the south side of Antero scars the landscape.

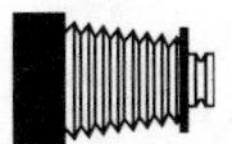

Grand Slam: 67, 72, 73, BC
54 Highest: 28

Jennings Creek ■

Elevation Gain: **4700 feet** Distance: **7 miles**

Continue 3 miles past the Angel of Shavano campground to Jennings Creek, 10,522 feet. This is the most popular route with a large sign at the trailhead warning of the strenuous route ahead.

Follow the trail through the aspen to timberline and continue east to gain the south spur of Tabeguache's west summit. Stay on this ridge until just before the west summit then circle to the east on the ridge to Tabeguache. Descend east to the saddle, 13,700 feet, and then up the ridge SE to Shavano. To descend, retrace your route over Tabeguache or continue south into McCoy Creek Basin. The McCoy descent has its hazards. Avoid following McCoy Creek to the road, rather cross it at timberline to the ridge west of the creek. Descend the steep timbered south facing slope to the road then hike up the road to the trailhead.

Angel of Shavano / Colorado Trail ■

Elevation Gain: **6000 feet** Distance: **12 miles**

Starting from the Angel of Shavano trailhead, 9200 feet, 3.5 miles north of US-50 along Chaffee County 240.

Hike 2 miles NE to where the Colorado Trail departs the Angel of Shavano trail. Follow the Angel of Shavano trail WNW to the summit of Shavano. This is the gully that forms the Angel of Shavano, a distinctive snowfield, in the early summer. Descend NW to the saddle, 13,700 feet, then west to the summit of Tabeguache. Retrace your route over Shavano for the descent.

McCoy Creek ◆

Elevation Gain: **4500 feet** Distance: **6 miles**

McCoy Creek is 5.5 miles north of US-50 on Chaffee County 240. Drive NW past McCoy Creek several hundred yards to park.

Climb north up the steep, rocky slopes to the ridge west of the creek. Once on the ridge, bushwhack to timberline. Pick your favorite steep talus slope to the summit of Tabeguache. Circle over to Shavano and then descend SW back to the ridge route west of McCoy Creek. No 'wimps or whiners' on this route.

Browns Creek ●

Elevation Gain: **3100 feet** Distance: **7 miles**

This route requires a backpack up Browns Creek from Chaffee County 272 or taking the Baldwin Gulch 4WD road from Chalk Creek (see Antero). From timberline NW of Tabeguache's summit head due south on a grassy slope to the west ridge of Tabeguache. Follow the ridge east to Tabeguache. Continue east from the summit to the saddle then SE to Shavano's summit. There are two choices for the down climb:

1. Retrace your route over Tabegauche's summit.
2. Go back to the saddle and go due north toward Browns Creek. The second alternative is steep and loose with no route markers. Expect steep snow fields early in summer.

Castle Peak

14,265

From the Top: If you climb Castle on the east ridge, just before reaching the height of the connecting saddle between Castle and Conundrum, the balance of the Elks will dramatically appear. Each of the fourteeners can be brought up close by a moderate telephoto lense. From left to right are Maroon, North Maroon, Snowmass, Capitol, and Pyramid. The gray-white monzonite of Snowmass and Capitol contrast with maroon formation rocks.

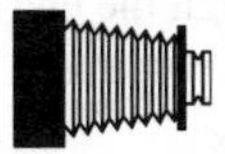

Grand Slam: 77
54 Highest: 47

Ashcroft ■

Elevation Gain: **4100 feet** Distance: **10 miles**

From Aspen drive west on CO-162 to the second stoplight after crossing Castle Creek. Turn south and immediately turn left onto Castle Creek Road. Drive south 11 miles to the restored ghost town of Ashcroft. Continue south 2 more miles and take the right fork at mile marker 13.

This ever rougher road crosses Castle Creek, 10,200 feet, in 1.2 miles. 1.5 miles past the creek is the Pearl Pass turnoff, 11,200 feet. Stay on the main road NW and in 2 miles is the end of the 4WD road, high, 12,200 feet, in Montezuma Basin.

Two choices exist from here, both start by gaining a natural bench 500 feet up a steep snowfield. From the bench the summit is visible to the left and you can go left or straight. The left choice has a great trail leading to a rocky ridge with minor exposure and great views. The straight choice requires scaling the saddle, 13,800 feet, between Castle and Conundrum. The very steep, hard snow field is a potential threat. More than one climber has lost hide sliding, unexpected, down the ice.

Aspen to Maroon Lake Campground

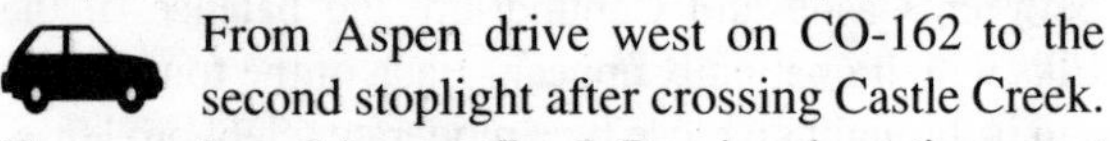

From Aspen drive west on CO-162 to the second stoplight after crossing Castle Creek. Turn south on Maroon Creek Road and continue past Aspen Highlands ski area. Drive SW 10 miles to and through the Maroon Lake campground to a high parking lot, 9,750 feet, on the west side.

The Maroon Creek road is closed every day from mid-June to Labor Day and weekends through the end of September, 8:30 AM to 5 PM so plan accordingly. Bus service is available during closed hours.

Pyramid Peak

14,018

From the Top: Surrounded by a sea of high mountains, the view depends on the time of day and hence the direction of the light. The steep east face of the Bells is worth studying particularly if you have yet to climb them. Looking further west over Buckskin Pass are Snowmass and Capitol. To the east is an unbroken string of fourteeners in the Sawatch. Identifying them is very difficult due to a lack of familiar landmarks.

Grand Slam: 74, 80
54 Highest: 40

Maroon Lake Campground ◆

Elevation Gain: **4300 feet** Distance: **6.5 miles**

From the high parking lot hike SW past the lake about one mile, when the trail opens up in a 'moonscape' of talus turn left and make your way to the steep chutes at the base of the peak. These steep tree-walled chutes lead to the high rock amphitheater, 11,600 feet, due north of the summit. From the amphitheater continue south to the north wall and choose left or right.

The left route gains the obvious saddle, 13,000 feet, on Pyramid's NE rib. From the saddle contour up and south on the east face to the summit.

The right route gains a buff-colored area, 12,800 feet, on the NW rib then zigzags up the west face to the summit.

These brief descriptions are necessary because of the complicated nature of the upper routes. Look for cairns, previous foot paths, and have the sense to retrace your steps if a choice will not "go." Pyramid's summit is surprisingly large and flat with cliffs all around.

North Maroon Peak

14,014

From the Top: Look northeast to Maroon Lake and imagine the first time you saw the Bells and wondered if anyone could ever climb such a steep mountain. With binoculars you can see hundreds of scurrying tourists; perhaps some of them have binoculars and are watching the crazy climbers on the summit.

Grand Slam: 78, 79, 81
54 Highest: 46

Maroon Lake Campground ♦♦

Elevation Gain: **4300 feet** Distance: **8 miles**

From the parking lot hike SW 2 miles to the Minnehaha Gulch / Buckskin Pass trail just before Crater Lake, 10,076 feet. Follow this trail west gaining roughly 800 feet to a large boulder and a faint left fork. The left fork drops down to Minnehaha Creek and crosses to a trail which climbs the willow-covered cliffs on the south side of the creek. Once on top of the cliffs, continue south on tundra to a large red, rock-glacier. Cross the rock to a modest notch, 11,800 feet, in the east rib of North Maroon. This notch has an easy trail which goes south and up to the major east gully. Turn around and take some bearings for the return. Head up the middle of this gully to the base of a major buff cliff, 12,800 feet. Contour south along the base of these cliffs past the next rib and into the gully. Go up this gully to the edge of the north face. Stay more or less on the east ridge to the summit.

Maroon Peak

14,156

From the Top: If you just did the traverse, you need no more views for this day. If not, then enjoy Fravert Basin to the southwest and the beautiful maroon and green patchwork as flora and rock create infinite patterns.

Grand Slam: 78, 79
54 Highest: 46

Maroon Lake Campground ♦

Elevation Gain: **4500 feet** Distance: **9 miles**

From the parking lot hike past Crater Lake and continue south for a total of 4 miles. A broad, steep, grassy, east facing, slope is the objective. Just before the trail crosses West Maroon Creek, 10,500 feet, head west and gain the ridge, 13,300 feet. Go north on the ridge and over the 13,753 SE summit of Maroon to a distinct saddle, 13,650 feet. Contour south around the cliff and find a comfortable gully to regain Maroon's SE ridge. Once back to the ridge the route is comparatively easy.

Maroon—North Maroon Ridge ♦♦

Elevation Gain: **300 feet** Distance: **.5 mile**

Supposedly going south to north is the easier direction, I've only done north to south. Descend north staying on the ridge to the saddle. A steep cliff north of the saddle has a climbable crack, go up it. Either stay on the ridge or favor the west side for a complicated series of ledges to North Maroon. For the north to south folks, the descent of the cliff to the saddle is the major problem as well as the steep, loose north ridge to Maroon's summit. Allow 2 hours and Good Luck!!!

Capitol Peak

14,130

From the Top: Look north at your approach and remember your thoughts. Capitol Lake is just below, and when you were there you wanted to be on top. Now that you are on top, you wish to sit on the lake's serene shores. Looking a little left you see the twin summits of Mount Sopris with buckskin and red-colored mountains between. Glance over to Snowmass and the picturesque parabolic ridges which connect these summits. Below to the left is the rugged Pierre Lakes Basin with its many shimmering lakes.

Grand Slam: 82, 83, RF
Pocket Slam: FC
54 Highest: 42, 43, 48-49

Capitol Creek ♦♦

Elevation Gain: **5000 feet** Distance: **14 miles**

From the town of Snowmass, on CO-162, turn south on a paved road following Snowmass Creek. Drive 1.7 miles until the road tees and turn right. Follow the right fork SW 8 miles to the trailhead at 9400 feet.

The trailhead is easily recognized by the fabulous view of Capitol Peak, 6 miles south. Two trails parallel Capitol Creek:

High Route

Go a few hundred feet SW along the ridge until an old irrigation ditch leads high and flat around the west side of the valley.

Low Route

Descend 400 feet to the creek below and follow a trail on the east side. Both trails merge after 3 miles. Continue south to a ring of trees just north of Capitol Lake, 11,600 feet, to camp.

Climb to the obvious saddle, 12,550 feet, just south of Mount Daly. Either stay on the ridge all the way to K2 or follow a trail SE dropping into the basin to take a snow and rock route to K2, 13,664 feet. The ridge route to K2 is more difficult than the knife edge but good rock and outrageous views more than compensate.

For the uninitiated, K2 is a prominent sub-peak on the ridge just before the knife edge. Neither of these features appear on the maps, they are just part of climbing legend.

Either go over K2 or circle around the west side to the ridge beyond. A couple hundred more yards is the knife edge. If the knife edge psyches you, a more difficult, less exposed route exists east and below the ridge. Continue on the ridge until it gets too steep then contour left to Capitol's SE ridge and circle around the south side to the summit.

Snowmass Mountain

14,092

From the Top: The small top is steep on both sides and provides excellent views of two valleys. Southwest is Geneva Lake more than 3000 feet below. Siberia Lake is up the same valley. The east side is dominated by the namesake snowfield, except in late summer when the gray-white monzonite is revealed. The Bells are only five miles away and all but unrecognizable because of the unfamiliar view. Notice how North Maroon appears as an insignificant bump on Maroon Peak's north ridge.

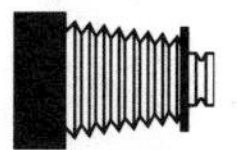

Grand Slam: 84, 85, RF
54 Highest: 3, 44-45, 48-49

Snowmass Lake ■

Elevation Gain: **5600 feet** Distance: **21 miles**

From the town of Aspen drive 5 miles NW, on CO-162, and turn SW at the Snowmass Village Road. Drive 6 miles, past the rodeo grounds and ski area, to a natural saddle separating Brush Creek from Snowmass Creek. A dirt road continues 1.8 miles down the NW side of the ski area to the trailhead, 8560 feet, at Snowmass Falls Ranch.

Another choice for this trailhead is to start at Snowmass on CO-162, not to be confused with Snowmass Village (the ski area), as if doing Capitol.

At the tee turn left and drive along Snowmass Creek 8.6 miles to where it joins the Snowmass Village Road. Turn right for another .2 mile to the trailhead.

From the trailhead hike on the east side of Snowmass Creek 8 miles to Snowmass Lake, 10,980 feet, to camp. Circle around the south side of the lake and head west up to the namesake snow basin. Angle SW to the saddle, 13,400 feet, between Snowmass Mountain and Hagerman Peak, 13,841 feet. Follow the ridge NW to the summit.

Lead King Basin ◆

Elevation Gain: **4400 feet** Distance: **8 miles**

From the town of Marble drive 2 miles east to a road fork. The left fork follows Lost Trail Creek and drops into Lead King Basin from the west after 4 miles of 4WD road. The right fork leads to Crystal in 3.5 miles then turns north for 2 more miles of exceptionally rough 4WD road to the trailhead, 9700 feet.

From the trailhead parking lot hike north on a good trail to Geneva Lake, 10,936 feet, for a great view of Snowmass and Hagerman.

Two climbing routes exist:

1. Follow the trail on the west side of the valley to Siberia Lake, 11,850 feet and go up the west ridge on large solid boulders. This will put you on the north summit with a slightly exposed quarter-mile to the true summit.

2. Circle around the lake and climb to the saddle, 13,400 feet, between Snowmass and Hagerman via the obvious gully east of the picturesque south ridge.

No trails exist for either of these choices . . . kind of like a pioneer!

San Luis Peak

14,014

From the Top: Creede, one of Colorado's legendary gold mining towns, is less than ten miles south, just across the Continental Divide. The divide is the soft ridge stretching east-west, less than two miles south of the summit. Due north is Gunnison, less than forty miles away. Uncompahgre Peak, thirty miles west, is always identifiable from any high southwestern summit.

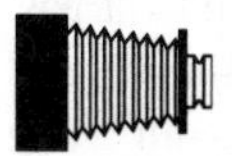

Grand Slam: 88
54 Highest: 69

There are two tricks to climbing San Luis: 1) Finding the trailhead and 2) Not climbing nearby Stewart Peak, 13,983 feet, by mistake. The trailhead can be reached from two different compass points.

Lake City–FS-794

Drive south out of Lake City on CO-149 heading for Creede. When the road tops out on Slumgullion Pass take FS-788 east to Cathedral, 15 miles. Just after crossing Cebolla Creek, 788 makes a right turn and 5 miles later joins FS-790, one mile past Los Pinos Pass, 10,514 feet. Turn right onto FS-790 and drive 8 miles to FS-794.

Doyleville–FS-794

From the summit of Monarch Pass continue west for 22 miles to Doyleville, take Gunnison County 45 south and then SW, 17 miles to intersect with CO-114. At 114 travel south for less than a half mile and turn right on the Old Agency road. Another 3.5 miles south and a right turn will put you on FS-790. About 9 miles

SW, FS-788 forks from 790, take the left fork staying on 790. Ahead 8 miles, just after Big Blue Park, will be the junction with FS-794.

FS-794–Stewart Creek

Head south on 794 for 8 miles, passing in order Pauline, Perfecto, Chavez, and Nutras Creeks. Take care not to follow 794 as it loops back NE along Chavez Creek. The road drops down to the Stewart Creek trailhead at 10,500 feet.

Stewart Creek ●

Elevation Gain: **3600 feet** Distance: **11 miles**

After getting here the route couldn't be easier. Hike west, about 4 miles, up Stewart Creek trail until timberline. Ahead is San Luis' prominent east false summit. Circle to the left of the false summit and find a decent trail to the ridge beyond. A mile-long ridge walk will put you on the summit. This is prime elk country and chances are good of spotting a herd anywhere including high above timberline.

San Luis Pass ●

Elevation Gain: **3900 feet** Distance: **14 miles**

Starting from Creede, CO-149, drive west on FS-517 past the cemetery about 3 miles. The road will climb steadily and turn north on an open hillside. After a couple of miles look on the left for FS-505. The Rio Grande Forest map is a considerable aid to finding these roads.

Follow FS-505 north 8 miles to San Luis Pass, 12,000 feet. This 4WD road is generally easy with several mud bogs—beware.

From San Luis Pass, hike east 5 miles on the Continental Divide ridge to the north-south connecting ridge to San Luis Peak. Follow the connecting ridge north 2 miles to the summit.

San Juan Range

Uncompahgre Peak

14,309

From the Top: The highest summit in the greater San Juan region has a commanding view. Surprisingly it is not easy to identify fourteeners to the south. This is owing to the uncommon height of all the lesser peaks. To the west, Wetterhorn, Sneffels and the two Wilsons are easy marks. Hike north from the true summit a couple hundred feet for a great view of the northeast face looking down into Nellie Creek. The summit has ample flowers in July for your enjoyment.

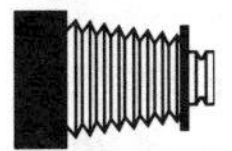

Grand Slam: 90, 92
54 Highest: 62, 64-65

Nellie Creek ■

Elevation Gain: **5000 feet** Distance: **13 miles**

From Lake City, CO-149, turn west on the Engineer Pass/Henson Creek road, Second Street. It's 5 miles to Nellie Creek at 9,310 feet.

An easy 4WD road follows Nellie Creek for 2.1 miles before it crosses the creek, 10,300 feet. After the creek crossing a rougher 4WD road continues another 1.7 miles to the trailhead.

From the Big Blue Wilderness trailhead, 11,500 feet, travel NW to timberline for your first close-up view of Uncompahgre's precipitous east face. The trail will lead you below the face and then around to the SE ridge. At 13,400 feet a large gap will open in the ridge for a great view of Wetterhorn. Looking over its summit, Sneffels is visible. The only route problem is at 13,900 feet, after gaining the high ridge and ring of cliffs. For a brief time the route goes to the west side and continues up one of several short steep gullies. At the top of the gullies an easy trail continues to the summit.

Matterhorn Creek ■

Elevation Gain: **3900 feet** Distance: **13 miles**

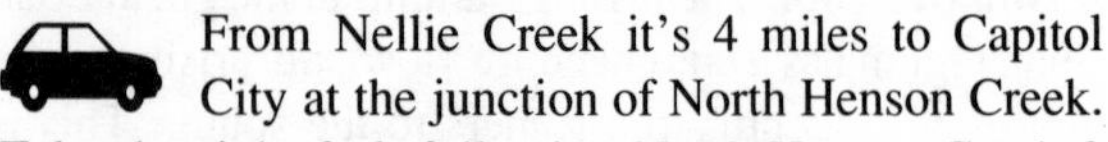

From Nellie Creek it's 4 miles to Capitol City at the junction of North Henson Creek. Take the right fork following North Henson Creek 2 miles to Matterhorn Creek, 10,400 feet.

Just before Matterhorn Creek a rough road follows the creek NE .7 mile to the trailhead.

From the trailhead, 11,000 feet, follow a closed road that leads north through tall timber along the creek. After 15 minutes, high cliffs due north will dominate the valley. This is the south ridge of Wetterhorn with the summit visible above and left. The road leads to a high bench to the east of these cliffs. Once onto the bench, the valley opens into a broad grassy expanse between Uncompahgre and Wetterhorn. Continue north on the road along the east side of Matterhorn Creek and stay on the road as it leads you high and east to gain Uncompahgre's SE ridge. Finish by using the balance of the Nellie Creek route. A high descent over to Wetterhorn can save some elevation gain if you plan on both summits for the day. The saddle between the two drops to 12,400 feet. Many camping opportunities exist in this valley.

Wetterhorn Peak

14,015

From the Top: Steep on all sides with a surprisingly large grassy summit from which the views are endless. Particularly interesting is the distinctive Cimarron

Range to the west. A number of drainages have their headwaters around Wetterhorn. These same drainages often have hiking trails which can be seen from the summit.

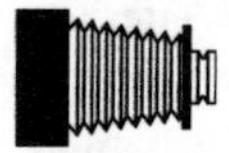

Grand Slam: 91
54 Highest: 64-65

Matterhorn Creek ◆

Elevation Gain: **3700 feet** Distance: **8 miles**

See Uncompahgre to get to the trailhead, 11,000 feet. From the trailhead, follow a closed road that leads north through tall timber along the creek. After 15 minutes, high cliffs due north will dominate the valley. This is the south ridge of Wetterhorn with the summit visible above and left. Spend a few minutes here studying the valley to the west of the cliffs. You may wish to descend this way on your return. Continue on the road as it leads to a high bench east of the cliffs. Once onto the bench the valley opens into a broad grassy expanse between Uncompahgre and Wetterhorn. Continue north on the road along the east side of Matterhorn Creek until it abruptly turns up and east and cross the creek to the west side.

Continue heading north towards Matterhorn Peak until Wetterhorn's summit appears on the left. Make a long sweeping U-turn to gain Wetterhorn's south ridge, 13,100 feet, on a NE facing grassy slope. Head north on the ridge until it becomes too steep and then contour along the west side until the prominent point just before the summit. Circle right around the point to a platform, 13,850 feet, between the point and summit. Take a deep breath! The last 200 feet to the summit is a series of steep steps, left of the platform, on top of a bottomless cliff. Kind of takes your breath away. Are we having fun now!!!

Redcloud Peak

14,034

From the Top: The most striking view is the vivid red rock on the summit with the twin towers of Wetterhorn and Uncompahgre in the distance. To the south across the Continental Divide is the prominent Rio Grande Pyramid.

Grand Slam: 86, 94, 95
54 Highest: 68

Sunshine Peak

14,001

From the Top: See how many old mining roads you can spot from this summit. Carson, a ghost town, is but five miles southeast, just below the Continental Divide.

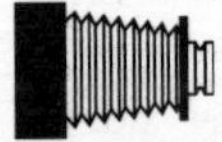

Grand Slam: 86, 94, 95
54 Highest: 68

Silver Creek ■

Elevation Gain: **4200 feet** Distance: **8.5 miles**

From Lake City travel south on CO-149 2.2 miles to the Cinnamon Pass/Lake San Cristobal turnoff, Hinsdale County 30, and head SW. It's paved to the west side of the lake and a good gravel road goes to the Sherman town site, for a total of 12 miles. At Sherman a steep, but well graded road leads around the south side of Sunshine on a marvel of road building. See if you can spot the old car used to stabilize the soil on one of the narrow ledges. Although the road is marked 4WD the Hinsdale County road crews do too good of a job to keep all but low clearance vehicles away. From Sherman it's 3.8 miles to Silver Creek, 10,400 feet.

Hike NE along the west side of Silver Creek 4 miles to the opposite side of Redcloud. At 12,800 feet you will gain the saddle between Redcloud and its eastern neighbor for a mostly firm trail to the summit. This seemingly long route is to avoid all the loose scree of these peaks.

From Redcloud travel south along the ridge noting the descent cairn at the saddle, 13,500 feet, as you make Sunshine's summit. Return to the cairn and descend west to the South Fork of Silver Creek. Follow this creek until it joins the main fork and trail. Two unnamed Century peaks are ENE of Redcloud, the first 13,832 feet is 1.5 miles and the second 13,811 feet is 2.5 miles away.

Handies Peak

14,048

From the Top: Twenty miles to the south are the Needle Mountains and Grenadier Range. Arrow and Vestal in the Grenadiers are the most spectacular with Pigeon Peak at the west end of the Needles also prominent. Closer is a steep headwall just above Sloan Lake at the south end of American Basin. If you look east between Redcloud and Sunshine, San Luis Peak appears as a bump on the horizon.

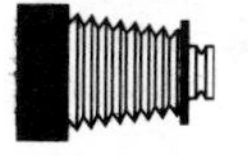

Grand Slam: 96, 97
54 Highest: 66, 67

American Basin ●

Elevation Gain: **2500 feet** Distance: **5 miles**

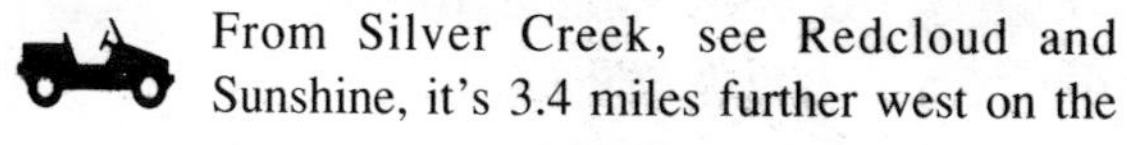

From Silver Creek, see Redcloud and Sunshine, it's 3.4 miles further west on the

Cinnamon Pass Road to American Basin. American Basin is one of the legendary San Juan flower locales. The Columbine cover the hillsides along with Indian Paintbrush, both red and ivory. From the turnoff into the basin, the road continues about a mile to 11,600 feet. Handies is on the left, east. Hike up the closed road which circles around Handies' SW side. Contour up the SW side to the summit.

Grizzly Gulch ●

Elevation Gain: **3600 feet** Distance: **6 miles**

The trailhead, 10,400 feet, is directly across the road from Silver Creek, see Redcloud and Sunshine. Hike SW across the Lake Fork of the Gunnison River and follow a good trail through the timber. The summit will be visible when the trail crosses a large boulder talus slope. Past the talus are grassy slopes to the ridge and then to the summit.

Sneffels Range

Mount Sneffels

14,150

From the Top: The blue-green waters of the Blue Lakes shimmer 3000 feet below. Up the other side of this compact valley is Dallas Peak, Colorado's hardest Century peak. Twenty miles away is the imposing bulk of Uncompahgre Peak. Notice how Wetterhorn Peak is framed by the larger, slightly more distant Uncompahgre.

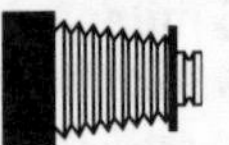

Grand Slam: 2, 100, 101
54 Highest: 74

Yankee Boy Basin ◆

Elevation Gain: **3100 feet** Distance: **4.5 miles**

From Ouray drive south on US-550 to the Box Canyon–Camp Bird–Yankee Boy Basin turnoff, Ouray County 361. Drive SW and then NW up a steep, improved gravel road 8 miles to timberline in Yankee Boy Basin.

At this point the road, if it wasn't already, is 4WD. Looking west the buff colored east face of Gilpin Peak dominates the valley. A steep 4WD road continues as high as 12,500 further west.

A foot trail roughly parallels the road to the trailhead. Follow a very good trail as if you were going over Blue Lakes Pass, to the west. Important, do not turn north until just before the Blue Lakes Pass switchbacks. Shortly before the switchbacks, a broad, steep gully on the right leads to a high saddle, 13,500 feet. At the saddle look west for a steeper gully, often snow filled, just south of the east ridge. Just before the top of the second gully exit left for the last 100 feet to the summit.

Blue Lakes ◆

Elevation Gain: **5600 feet** Distance: **10 miles**

Starting at Ridgeway, US-550 and CO-62, drive west 5 miles on 62 to the Dallas Creek road, Ouray County 7. Drive south 2 miles and turn right at a road fork. Continue 7 more miles to the wilderness boundary and trailhead, 9,200 feet.

Backpack to the lakes, 11,000 feet, to camp. From your camp continue over Blue Lakes Pass, 13,000 feet, to pick up the above route. The lakes can be seen from the summit. The drive up the East Dallas Creek road will allow you to see the locales for most of the Sneffels calendar photos.

San Miguel Mountains

Wilson Peak

14,017

From the Top: Looking over the south ridge of Wilson Peak are the triple summits of Gladstone, Mount Wilson and El Diente with Navajo Basin below the ridge. Further right is Navajo Pass and Silver Pick Basin. To the north is Wilson Mesa which abruptly drops into the San Miguel River. Across the river are the south slopes of the Sneffels Range with Mount Sneffels further to the right. The twisting slopes of the Telluride Ski Area are visible to the northeast. Ophir Pass can be located by the road which crosses the west face of Lookout Peak. Further right is the volcanic plug of Lizard Head Peak. Between Lizard Head and Wilson Peak is Bilk Basin. See if you can spot the small cabin high in Bilk Basin.

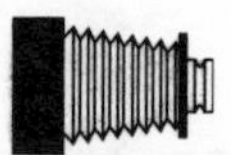

Grand Slam: 8-9, 98, 103
54 Highest: 78

Silver Pick Basin ◆

Elevation Gain: **3100 feet** Distance: **5 miles**

National Forest Access, Silver Pick Road goes south from CO-145 6.4 miles SE of Placerville, junction of CO's 62 and 145. This good gravel road forks after 3.1 miles of picturesque red rock canyon. Continue on the left fork 0.7 miles to another junction. Turn right and drive 3.7 miles south to the Silver Pick Mill trailhead, 10,900 feet.

Depending on your vehicle and the snow conditions it is possible to 4WD as high as 12,140 feet, the collapsed ruins of the Silver Pick Mine rock bunk house. This 4WD road is very rocky and only takes 1.5 miles to gain the 1,200 feet.

Most people stop at the mill. In any case the road/trail continues south to Navajo Pass 13,000 feet. The trail degrades significantly after the bunk house but is still better than the loose scree.

Once at Navajo Pass look east to survey the last 1000 feet. The easiest choice is to circle south and east of Wilson Peak's south buttress and regain the ridge at the prominent notch. From the pass hike east on the ridge then south of the buttress to the east side of the Wilson Peak–Gladstone ridge, gaining about 200 feet. From the east side go north and gain the ridge by heading for the notch. From the notch, follow an obvious ridge path to a point looking down into a NW gully. A quick glance at the ridge will convince you that the gully is the lesser of two evils. Drop about 50 feet into the gully and contour up and north on the west side of the ridge. This gully is steep and will be icy in early summer as well as after Labor Day. Once back to the ridge the summit is a short stroll ahead.

Bilk Basin ◆

Elevation Gain: **4300 feet** Distance: **11 miles**

Take National Forest Access, South Fork Road 2.0 miles SE as it follows the South Fork to Illium. At a new bridge, marked 63L and 63J, cross the river to the west side and follow the old railroad grade south 2.9 miles until it dead-ends and follow a steeper graded dirt road up and west.

The road tees after 0.6 miles where the left fork, 4WD recommended, continues 1.4 miles and climbs to a meadow, 9,700 feet, with a beautiful view of Wilson Peak. The road crosses the east edge of the meadow past several old buildings into the timber and continues several more miles to Bilk Creek, 10,050 feet. Caution, past the meadow the road is very muddy but an easy hike.

Cross Bilk Creek and follow the trail south along the west side of the creek. This is the Lizard Head Wilderness Area. Follow the trail past where it crosses Bilk Creek's west fork at 11,400 feet. Take the right fork of the trail west to a miners cabin at 13,000 feet, just below the Wilson Peak–Gladstone ridge. Climb west to the ridge and pick up the balance of the Silver Pick route.

A somewhat shorter route to Upper Bilk Basin would be to start from 2 miles SW of Lizard Head Pass on CO-145, 10,000 feet. Hike north on a good trail over the ridge, 12,000 feet, at the base of Lizard Head, and drop down to the west fork of Bilk Creek.

Mount Wilson

14,246

From the Top: Wilson's small steep summit permits bird-like looks all around. The steep permanent snowfield east of the summit is one of the last remaining in Colorado. How long before it disappears and becomes seasonal? The rocky rubble of Kilpacker Basin is to the west, with the connecting ridge to El Diente slightly to the north. Looking north you will see Navajo Pass and Wilson Peak. Further right is Sneffels, just left of Gladstone.

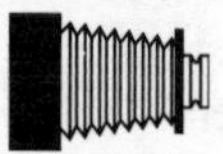

Grand Slam: 105, 112
54 Highest: FC, 79

El Diente Peak

14,159

From the Top: Look south to see Dunton Meadows just past the tree-covered ridge. Kilpacker Creek is just below El Diente and flows into the West Dolores River. From left to right Dolores Peak, Lone Cone and Little Cone are visible. The western horizon reveals the blue-gray outline of Utah's La Sal Mountains.

Grand Slam: 104, 105
54 Highest: 5, 76, RF

Navajo Pass ♦♦

Elevation Gain: **3700 feet** Distance: **4 miles**

From Navajo Pass (see Wilson Peak) Mount Wilson and El Diente are just across upper Navajo Basin. Descend south 700 feet toward Mount Wilson then up the grassy rib on the right of the prominent snow-filled gully, between Gladstone and Wilson. Before reaching the ridge contour right to a 14,000 foot saddle NE of the summit. Mount Wilson's summit is gained via a series of benches which go up the NE cliff face in a small gully.

Return to Navajo Basin

To return to upper Navajo Basin from El Diente follow the ridge east to the reddish saddle just west of the Organ Pipes. Descend due north and pick your way down the steep, cliff strewn, north face.

Navajo Lake and Kilpacker Creek

From Lizard Head Pass, 10,222 feet, continue SW on CO-145 6 miles to the Dunton Road. Follow this dirt road 6 miles to Dunton meadows or The Meadows on some maps. A small group of large spruce define the trailhead, 10,050 feet.

Navajo Lake ♦♦

Elevation Gain: **5700 feet** Distance: **16 miles**

From The Meadows El Diente's summit is visible NE over the gentle forested hill. Backpack west across the meadows and then north for 2.5 miles until reaching Kilpacker Creek. The trail descends to Kilpacker Creek and the West Dolores River and continues for 3 miles around the west side of El Diente's west ridge to Navajo Lake, 11,154 feet.

Look east up the basin for a large boulder resting on a ridge that runs to El Diente's summit. Hike to this boulder and follow the ridge SE to the summit.

Kilpacker Creek ♦

Elevation Gain: **5200 feet** Distance: **13 miles**

Backpack west across the meadows and then north for 2.5 miles until reaching Kilpacker Creek. Just before dropping down to the creek, follow a faint old road along the south side of Kilpacker for a mile or until the creek turns back north. Cross the creek and free-form north toward El Diente's summit, staying west of the creek. Because of the largely open meadows this is easier than it appears. At timber's edge, the falls and summit are visible.

Circle west of the falls and go up and east on the scree to just east of El Diente. Take the red gully north to the ridge west of the Organ Pipes and turn west on the ridge to gain the summit.

Mount Wilson—El Diente Ridge

Two choices exist for the traverse between the two summits.

◆ 1. Descend south from Mount Wilson's summit about 100 feet to the first gully. Follow this gully NW to upper Kilpacker basin. Drop in total about 1000 feet and skirt south of the prominent cliffs. Continue west and diagonal up when the red gully is visible. Follow the red gully up to the ridge, west of the organ pipes. Stay on the ridge or go north around the ridge to El Diente.

If you are going from El Diente to Wilson note that finding the summit gully can be tricky. After descending the red gully into Kilpacker continue east and diagonal up when the three summits of Mount Wilson are visible. The triple summits are a perspective distortion. Head up the steep scree for the gully between the left pair of summits. When almost to the top of the gully, turn left up a steeper gully for the last hundred feet to the summit.

◆◆ 2. Stay on or just south of the connecting ridge skirting the Organ Pipes one-quarter-mile west of El Diente. This ridge is thin in places with less than ideal rock.

There are numerous ways to get to Chicago Basin, all involve considerable hiking, some add the mystique of a train ride.

Train Routes

The Durango & Silverton Narrow Gauge Railroad follows the Animas River. The steam trains carry you as a normal passenger and place your packs in a boxcar. Pets can ride the boxcar in an approved airline carrier. Not all of the trains drop passenger at Needleton, 8135 feet. Reservations are recommended for the busy summer months, call ahead for current times and fares. Lest you think that Needleton is a train station, picture a rail siding instead . . . no creature comforts here.

Be sure to bring some cash for the return trip—it's amazing the craving one gets for junk food after several days in Chicago Basin.

Season: Early May–Late October

Durango
Phone: 303-247-2733
Fare: $34

The second, not express, train leaves about 8:30 AM and drops passengers at Needleton sometime around 11 AM. The return to Durango is about 3 PM.

Silverton
Phone: 303-387-5416
Fare: $22

The last train to Durango will drop backpackers and leaves the station about 3 PM for the hour trip to Needleton. The return time is about 11 AM.

Hiking Access

Needleton to Chicago Basin

Elevation Gain: **3000 feet** Distance: **6 miles**

From Needleton it is a half mile stroll south to Needle Creek and the Weminuche Wilderness boundary. Backpack up the old wagon road on the north side of Needle Creek. In 2 miles you will cross New York Creek and 4 more to Chicago Basin, at 11,000+ feet. Numerous campsites exist in the timber on either side of the creek. No camp fires are permitted in the Needle Creek drainage, just stoves. Strong parties may wish to camp at the twin lakes, 12,500 feet. The last 500 feet, to the lakes is very steep. Camping at the lakes will very likely be banned, due to severe overuse.

Columbine Pass

Elevation Gain: **4800 feet** Distance: **16 miles**

Start at the Weminuche Wilderness boundary, 8000 feet, several miles north of Vallecito Reservoir. Hike 8 miles north along Vallecito Creek to its junction, 9200 feet, with Johnson Creek. Follow this trail SW and then NW 6 miles to the top of Columbine Pass, 12,800 feet. Drop into Chicago Basin, 11,200 feet, to camp.

Purgatory to Needle Creek

Elevation Gain: **700 feet** Distance: **10 miles**

Starting at a lower Purgatory Ski Area parking lot, 8800 feet, cross US-550 to the Purgatory Campground entrance and trailhead. The Purgatory trail drops to Purgatory Flats, a beautiful meadow. Follow the trail SE to a narrow entrance to Cascade Creek Canyon. Gain several hundred feet as you skirt the canyon cliffs. Drop the remaining elevation to a new forest service bridge, 7700 feet, over the Animas River. Hike northeast on an abandoned road along the southeast side of the Animas for 7 miles to Needle Creek. Pick up the Chicago Basin trail after crossing Needle Creek.

Mount Eolus

14,083

From the Top: Look west for the best views. Much of the Animas River can be seen as a silver thread beneath great canyon walls. Purgatory Ski Area can be seen as a series of light green grassy slopes contrasting with the dark green forest. Nearby Pigeon Peak is the most prominent of the Needle Mountains and the fourth highest.

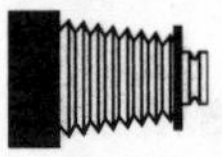

Grand Slam: 108, 109, 112, BC
54 Highest: 73

Chicago Basin ◆

Elevation Gain: **3000 feet** Distance: **3 miles**

Go south of the large buttress that is just west of the lakes and find a grass-fringed trail heading straight for Eolus. The true summit is just north of the prominent notch in the ridge. The trail will lead you to a rock wall with a diagonal ramp which heads up and east. This will put you on a gravel bench for a short distance as you circle back to the west. The summit of North Eolus will be visible high to the right. Head up a series of ledges to the saddle, 13,850 feet. Eolus' summit will be visible SW with a long connecting ridge between. This is known as the Sidewalk in the Sky. The rock is solid as well as the footing, so enjoy the view. There are at least three summit routes after the sidewalk. In increasing order of difficulty they are:

◆ 1. Contour along the east face and move aggressively up a series of steep ledges directly to the summit.
◆ 2. Contour up the east face on a well traveled series of benches under the summit and circle back encountering one difficult crack.
◆◆ 3. Take the scenic summit ridge. If you need directions, don't use this choice.

Sunlight Peak

14,059

From the Top: Sunlight has two tops, the highest point which is a large plate leaning against a rounded boulder; and the more ordinary rock summit 50 feet south which has the USGS benchmark. To the north are the twin summits of Arrow and Vestal, the monarches of the Grenadiers. Far to the east is the lonesome Rio Grande Pyramid. Below are glacier-carved lakes in the high-alpine Sunlight Basin.

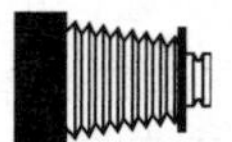

Grand Slam: 106, 110
54 Highest: 72

Chicago Basin ◆

Elevation Gain: **3000 feet** Distance: **3 miles**

Hike east of the twin lakes to about the miners cabin. Head east into the glacier-scrubbed basin below Sunlight and Windom. Ascend the red gully to the ridge, then staying on the west side of the ridge continue north on a series of ledges. At a large flat red ledge a hole in the wall will appear on the right, take a look. You're right, that's not the way. At the extreme left of the red ledge look for a cairn above a crack. Go up and circle west of a big boulder. If around the boulder is a flat plate which you have to crawl under, you made it!

The summit register is a flat stroll away. Hardy souls go for the summit rock just above the register. Return to the lakes for the trail to Eolus.

Windom Peak

14,082

From the Top: Southeast of the summit are several blue-green lakes in upper Grizzly Gulch. The near vertical east side of Windom induces some involuntary knee quiver. To the southwest the Chicago Basin is exposed with its trail system and infrequent mines.

Grand Slam: 106
54 Highest: 70

Chicago Basin ◆

Elevation Gain: **3000 feet** Distance: **3 miles**

From the glacier-scrubbed basin, see Sunlight, circle south to the saddle. This saddle is between the 13,400 foot summit which dominated the view from lower Chicago Basin and Windom's west ridge. Staying either on the ridge or slightly north, gain the top. A few quick moves to the south will put you on Windom's summit block. How about that 'get-off' on the east side! Beautiful green lakes down there too. To climb Sunlight, descend part way down the west ridge and take a steep scree gully north.

Climbing Notes

Fourteeners by Difficulty

Very Difficult ♦♦

Mount Wilson	14,246	Little Bear Peak	14,037
Crestone Needle	14,197	North Maroon Pk	14,014
Capitol Peak	14,130		

Difficult ♦

Crestone Peak	14,294	Mount Eolus	14,083
Longs Peak	14,255	Windom Peak	14,082
Kit Carson Mtn	14,165	Sunlight Peak	14,059
El Diente Peak	14,159	Pyramid Peak	14,018
Maroon Peak	14,156	Wilson Peak	14,017
Mount Sneffels	14,150	Wetterhorn Peak	14,015
Snowmass Mtn	14,092		

Moderate ■

Mount Harvard	14,420	Mount Oxford	14,153
Blanca Peak	14,345	Missouri Mtn	14,067
La Plata Peak	14,336	Humboldt Peak	14,064
Uncompahgre Pk	14,309	Ellingwood Point	14,042
Castle Peak	14,265	Mount Lindsey	14,042
Mount Shavano	14,229	Redcloud Peak	14,034
Mount Belford	14,197	Holy Cross	14,005
Mount Yale	14,196	Sunshine Peak	14,001
Mt Tabeguache	14,155		

Easy ●

Mount Elbert	14,433	Mount Democrat	14,148
Mount Massive	14,421	Pikes Peak	14,110
Mount Lincoln	14,286	Mount Columbia	14,073
Grays Peak	14,270	Mount Bierstadt	14,060
Mount Antero	14,269	Handies Peak	14,048
Torreys Peak	14,267	Culebra Peak	14,047
Quandary Peak	14,265	Mount Sherman	14,036
Mount Evans	14,264	San Luis Peak	14,014
Mount Princeton	14,197	Huron Peak	14,005
Mount Bross	14,172		

Fourteeners by Elevation

1	Elbert	14,433	28	Sneffels	14,150
2	Massive	14,421	29	Democrat	14,148
3	Harvard	14,420	30	Capitol	14,130
4	Blanca	14,345	31	Pikes	14,110
5	La Plata	14,336	32	Snowmass	14,092
6	Uncompahgre	14,309	33	Eolus	14,083
7	Crestone	14,294	34	Windom	14,082
8	Lincoln	14,286	35	Columbia	14,073
9	Grays	14,270	36	Missouri	14,067
10	Antero	14,269	37	Humboldt	14,064
11	Torreys	14,267	38	Bierstadt	14,060
12	Castle	14,265	39	Sunlight	14,059
12	Quandary	14,265	40	Handies	14,048
14	Evans	14,264	41	Culebra	14,047
15	Longs	14,255	42	Ellingwood	14,042
16	Mt Wilson	14,246	42	Lindsey	14,042
17	Shavano	14,229	44	Little Bear	14,037
18	Crestone Ndl	14,197	45	Sherman	14,036
18	Belford	14,197	46	Redcloud	14,034
18	Princeton	14,197	47	Pyramid	14,018
21	Yale	14,196	48	Wilson Pk	14,017
22	Bross	14,172	49	Wetterhorn	14,015
23	Kit Carson	14,165	50	N Maroon	14,014
24	El Diente	14,159	50	San Luis	14,014
25	Maroon	14,156	52	Huron	14,005
26	Tabeguache	14,155	52	Holy Cross	14,005
27	Oxford	14,153	54	Sunshine	14,001

① COLORADO 14'ers - GRAND SLAM

9 x 12 Format, 112 Pages, 90 Photos, 13 Color Maps. "**Grand Slam** . . . sparkles pictorially while providing solid information . . . 90 color photos, many of them spectacular" Charlie Meyers–Denver Post

③ COLORADO 14'ers - 54 HIGHEST

8 x 10-3/4 Format, 84 Pages, 56 Color Photographs. The first all color fourteener book, over 20,000 sold.

④ MAP SLAM

A complete list of fourteener maps organized by ranges; the list includes Forest Service, and USGS: 7.5′, 15′, and County maps. Printed on both sides of an 8.5 x 11 card.

⑤ LOG SLAM

An expanded version of the climbing log on pages 42 and 43, but with room for multiple climbs, dates, climbing companions, and notes. Printed on both sides of an 8.5 x 11 card.

FOURTEENER CALENDAR

In June 1992, look for the 1993 Fourteener Calendar with 14 all new color photographs of Colorado's highest mountains. Order directly from Above the Timber or your favorite retail book seller.

Autographing

All books can be personally autographed by Roger Edrinn. There is no additional charge for this courtesy. Please allow 2 weeks extra delivery time. Include name of recipient for the salutation and any special date if you wish more than month and year. Type or clearly print your instructions to avoid delays or errors.

⑦ SHIRT SLAM

A heavy weight cotton T-Shirt with all 54 fourteeners and their difficulty rankings on the front, see page 80. Each summit has a place to checkoff your climb with a fabric pen. The back design is shown below. Available in two colors: Light Blue and Hot Pink; and three sizes: M, L, and XL. Remember–children grow–so think big!

Above the Timber

2366 Wapiti Road

Fort Collins, CO 80525

Item	Description	Qty	Cost	Amount
①	Colorado 14'ers/**GRAND SLAM**		$19.95	
②	Colorado 14'ers **POCKET SLAM**		$5.95	
③	Colorado 14'ers *54 Highest Peaks*		$12.95	
④	**Map Slam**		$1.50	
⑤	**Log Slam**		$1.50	
⑥	**Slam Set** (Items ①②④⑤)		$25.00	
⑦	Grand Slam T–Shirt Size _____ Color __________		$19.95	

	Sub-Total	________
Colo residents add 3%	Sales Tax	________
Orders up to $25 add $3 Orders over $25 add $4	S&H	________
	Total	________

Check Money Order

Name ______________________________

Address ______________________________

City ____________________ State ________ Zip ________

Phone (   ) ______________________________

Best time to call?

Allow three weeks for delivery